PRAISE FOR james endredy

Ecoshamanism

Ecoshamanism is a must-have book for customers interested in ecology and shamanic spirituality.

—*New Age Retailer*

Endredy describes more than fifty ecoshamanic practices, including ceremonies, rituals, and chants, designed to provide connection to the spirit world and heal the earth...A hopeful and encouraging book.

—*Library Journal*

Beyond 2012

Leave it to James Endredy to write a book on 2012 that actually makes sense. I've liked what I've read of his work, particularly *Ecoshamanism* (which is one of my absolute favorite books on shamanism). *Beyond 2012* completely reframes the 2012 situation, focusing on rebuilding connectivity and awareness on a greater scale and offering people a variety of tools to choose from.

—*Lupa, Paganbookreviews.com*

As with Endredy's previous book, *Ecoshamanism, Beyond 2012* will appeal to those who are ready to explore ways to use personal power to help awaken others and to heal the earth.

—*New Age Retailer*

Lightning in My Blood

James Endredy carries the old tradition of sacred storyteller, which he shares in a masterful way in his new book. His writing takes you into his experience so you feel a part of what he speaks, what he feels, what he learns about and sees. He offers down-to-earth explanations of the medicine ways so readers can apply the practical teachings in their own lives. It is a good time to sit down in a quiet place and open to what James Endredy's writing can bring into your awareness: the wisdom of respect for the sacred mystery of life and all its creations, seen and unseen, which is precisely what we need more of during these challenging times of transition. Read and enjoy, learn and grow, share with your friends, and live a good life. This book will help you on your road.

—Dr. Tom Pinkson, author, *The Shamanic Wisdom of the Huichol: Medicine Teachings for Modern Times*

Lightning in My Blood is an extraordinary accomplishment, a powerful book of wonderful tales from James Endredy's life experience. Not only is he a compelling storyteller, but he is able to convey a great deal of useful information about the shamanic path through his magical tales. I highly recommend this book, both for the sheer fun of his humorous, harrowing stories and for its ability to carry you deeply into the world of the shaman.

—José Luis Stevens, PhD,
author of *Praying with Power*

Be forewarned: when you open this book, you step into a different world, a world of cosmic clowns and dwarf kings, of water spirits and blue deer. As Endredy writes, "the shaman takes the first step of his journey where most take their last," and here the journey of the traveler begins and doesn't end until our dream of reality becomes the reality of our dreams. Nervous? Don't be. Actually, do be nervous. But dive in anyway.

—Hillary S. Webb, author of *Traveling Between the Worlds: Conversations with Contemporary Shamans*

the
flying
witches
of veracruz

about the author

James Endredy is a teacher, mentor, and guide to thousands of people through his books and workshops. After a series of life tragedies and mystical experiences as a teenager, he changed direction from his Catholic upbringing and embarked on a lifelong spiritual journey to encounter the mysteries of life and death and why we are all here. For over twenty-five years, he has learned shamanic practices from all over the globe while also studying with kawiteros, lamas, siddhas, roadmen, and leaders in the modern fields of ecopsychology, bioregionalism, and sustainable living. James also worked for ten years with Mexican shamanic researcher Victor Sanchez, learning to share shamanic practices with modern people.

On a daily level, his experiences have inspired him to live a sustainable lifestyle as much as possible while still working within mainstream society. He writes, leads workshops, mentors private clients, visits schools and community centers, speaks at bookstores, and volunteers in his community. His books—including *Ecoshamanism* and *Beyond 2012*—have thus far been published in seven languages.

A Shaman's True
Story of Indigenous
Witchcraft, Devil's Weed,
and Trance Healing
in Aztec Brujería

the
flying
witches
of Veracruz

JAMES ENDREDY

Llewellyn Publications
WOODBURY, MINNESOTA

FIRST EDITION
First Printing, 2011

Book design by Rebecca Zins
Cover art © 2011 Eric Williams/Koralik Associates
Cover design by Kevin R. Brown
Interior flower image is from *Art Nouveau Floral Designs*
(©2005, Dover Publications) and Aztec images from Veracruz
are from *Design Motifs of Ancient Mexico* by Jorge Enciso
(©1953, Dover Publications)

Llewellyn Publications is a registered trademark
of Llewellyn Worldwide Ltd.

Library of Congress Cataloging-in-Publication Data
Endredy, James.
   The flying witches of Veracruz: a shaman's true story of indigenous witchcraft, devil's weed, and trance healing in Aztec brujería / James Endredy.—1st ed.
       p. cm.
   ISBN 978-0-7387-2756-1
   1. Hallucinogenic drugs and religious experience—Mexico—Veracruz-Llave (State) 2. Datura—Mexico—Veracruz-Llave (State) 3. Shamanism—Mexico—Veracruz-Llave (State) 4. Wicca—Mexico—Veracruz-Llave (State) 5. Endredy, James. 6. Trance—Mexico—Veracruz-Llave (State) I. Title.
   BL65.D7E53 2011
   201'.44097262—dc23
                                                         2011029479

Llewellyn Worldwide Ltd. does not participate in, endorse, or have any authority or responsibility concerning private business transactions between our authors and the public.

All mail addressed to the author is forwarded, but the publisher cannot, unless specifically instructed by the author, give out an address or phone number.

Any Internet references contained in this work are current at publication time, but the publisher cannot guarantee that a specific location will continue to be maintained. Please refer to the publisher's website for links to authors' websites and other sources.

Llewellyn Publications
A Division of Llewellyn Worldwide Ltd.
2143 Wooddale Drive
Woodbury, MN 55125-2989
www.llewellyn.com
Printed in the United States of America

contents

part 1

witches, spells, and consequences

part 2

flying, dreaming, and the devil's weed

part 3

dream-trance healing

warning

This book contains explicit material about experiences that occurred under the influence of the plant species *Datura inoxia*, *Datura stramonium*, and *Datura ceratocaula*, collectively known as devil's weed, jimsonweed, thorn apple, hell's bells, and devil's trumpet, among others. Along with nightshade, henbane, and mandrake, these plants have long been classified as "witches' weeds" due to their psychoactive effects and their use by witches cross-culturally.

Daturas grow wild in most places throughout the world and have also been cultivated for centuries for their beautiful flowers and their medicinal properties. However, without extensive experience and training, no one should ever ingest datura, and even the most highly experienced take great risk in doing so. Common reactions to ingesting the plant include extreme nausea; blurred or fixed-focus vision; rapid heartbeat; extreme drying and irritation of the mouth, throat, eyes, urinary tract, and other mucous membranes; extreme disorientation; loss of memory; delirium; loss of body control; extreme audio, visual, and tactile hallucinations; astral travel; uncontrollably emotional or violent activity; and even death.

Although these plants have been (and are still) used in cultures throughout the world for their medicinal value and use as an entheogen, they are not a part of our culture and should never be ingested. If someone wants to experiment with these plants, I suggest basking in the glory of their beautiful flowers and getting to know their power *without* ingestion. This is the only way I use them now.

As written in the introduction to this book, and as you will see as my story unfolds, I was originally given datura to ingest without my knowledge or consent. My subsequent actions were the result of being with experienced practitioners who knew how to cure me and how to use these powerful plants. But if I had not been given it without my knowledge, I would never have tried it.

Do not experiment with these plants; any contact with these plants could result in harm and even death. The material herein is not meant to encourage the use of datura; to do so would be completely irresponsible. This material is for informational and entertainment purposes only.

introduction

the phenomenal spread of Wicca and its many forms is documented today in studies such as the American Religious Identification Survey, which reports the number of Wiccans. This has doubled since 2001, and for good reason.

Authentic Wiccan spirituality has nothing to do with the devil or evildoing. On the contrary, Wiccans and shamans believe in and work with the "good" forces of nature. Persons of this nature tend to be pacifists, promote environmentalism and green lifestyles, balance equality between feminine and masculine, and in general are one the most peaceful and loving spiritual groups currently on the planet. Today, mainstream movies, shows, and books have utterly transformed the common perception of who witches are and what they do. Most people who want to learn more about the subject turn to the most popular and accessible form of witchcraft, generally known as Wicca;

however, true shamanism is at its best represented in the cultures authentic to this path.

Although I do not personally consider myself Wiccan, which is essentially a form of spirituality that was born in Europe and spread to the United States, I do greatly love my Wiccan friends and companions and share in many of their values. I have documented my path toward a similar lifestyle to Wicca in previous books such as *Earthwalks for Spirit* (Bear and Co., 2002), *Ecoshamanism* (Llewellyn, 2005), *Beyond 2012* (Llewellyn, 2008), and *Lightning in My Blood* (Llewellyn, 2011).

In *Lightning in My Blood*, I share twenty-five personal stories of supernatural and enlightening experiences with shamans, healers, and witches from across the globe. With the book you are now reading, I have expanded on one area of teachings specifically related to witchcraft. I have done this primarily in the hope of expanding the popular perception of witchcraft, especially for those only familiar with the Euro-American versions of Wicca and offshoots thereof. Wicca is only one in a pantheon of witchcraft practices throughout the world.

This book is a personal account of my experiences with witchcraft in the state of Veracruz, Mexico, and the rural Tuxtlas Mountains to the northwest of Catemaco. By no means is this a work of anthropological or ethnographical study. Quite the contrary; as my story unfolds, you will clearly see that although I did originally arrive at the region out of curiosity for the annual witchcraft festival, it was never my intention to remain in the area at that time or do any in-depth study of current witchcraft practices of the region. I was merely there to visit with some friends when I involuntarily became sucked into a vortex of supernatural witchcraft practices that underlie the cultural consciousness of the people in that area. Consequently, I was formally trained in an esoteric form of witchcraft by a small group of highly skilled witches.

That mysticism, magic, and witchcraft pervades the area of the Tuxtlas is hardly surprising given its past history. The prehistoric and mysterious Olmec civilization, famous for their colossal stone heads, inhabited the region from approximately 1500 BC to AD 300, after which the Teotihuacan people thrived in the area of Matacapan (15 km from Catemaco) and later built the massive pyramids and city of Teotihuacan to the northwest of the Tuxtlas. The Pyramid of the Sun, built by the Teotihuacans, is the third largest pyramid in the world. The Aztecs conquered the area next and reigned until the time of the Spaniards.

All of the pre-Columbian civilizations had at their core what modern people would refer to as magical or supernatural practices and beliefs. Even after Cortez and the Spanish missionaries decimated the native population, the magical systems continued, albeit covertly, and were gradually mixed with the magic-religious practices of the African slaves introduced to the area in the early 1500s. Today, the rural spiritualism of the area is a combination of Aztec *brujería*, African-Haitian Voudon, Cuban Santería, and Christianity.

As is the case with most of Mexico, the city and urban centers are predominantly Christian/Catholic based, and the farther one moves into rural areas, the more one encounters a mix between indigenous spiritual practices and Christianity. But in some areas of Mexico there still reside indigenous forms of spirituality that have almost entirely avoided Christian influence. My experiences with the witches of the Tuxtlas falls into this category, as there were absolutely no Christian practices or vocabulary employed by these practitioners. I would venture to say from my observations that this is not the norm for the area of Catemaco, Veracruz City, or Mexico in general. I believe the world of witches that I was thrust into to be a very specific and esoteric "tribe" whose practices have become nearly extinct. Moreover, the ritual use of datura was something I had never before encountered in over twenty years of traveling throughout Mexico and living with various indigenous groups.

In my previous books on shamanism, I have related ideas, facts, practices, and stories in an attempt to share and possibly educate the public on the concepts and sensible uses of shamanic knowledge in our modern world. This has proven to be an extremely enlightening process for myself as well. Each new experience or new comprehension then translated into the written word propels me deeper into the tasks of both researcher and facilitator.

With this latest book, I have deviated slightly in both terminology and practicality. With respect to terminology, I have found it necessary to accurately convey the following accounts and information under the auspices of witchcraft rather than shamanism simply due to the circumstances of the events, where they happened, and the terminology employed by my teachers. In the following account of my experiences with the flying witches of Veracruz, they themselves used the terms *witch* and *witchcraft* to describe themselves and what they were doing. However, I must make it clear that in the culture herein described, where the people speak Spanish and Nahuatl, the meanings of the English translation of the words *witchcraft* and *witch* do not necessarily correlate to what our culture perceives as witchcraft or witch.

In this sense, as also with the words *shaman* or *shamanism* in general, from the cultural perspective of the people of the Tuxtlas, there are good witches and evil witches—and even witches who are both. I am simply using the terms *witch* and *witchcraft* to describe the people and events in this book because they are the best English words I have to use. *Brujería* is the Spanish word that most closely translates to *witchcraft* in English. However, like the English term *witchcraft*, the Spanish word *brujería* is most commonly used to describe the evil or negative aspects and functions of the Craft, even though most people with interest in this topic would agree that there are both good witches and bad witches (good *brujos* and bad *brujos*).

In Spanish, the word *curandera* (female) or *curandero* (male) refers to a folk healer. In this context, there is no negative connotation associated with these practitioners. But in my experiences with the healers (good witches) described in this book, it became apparent that in order to be proficient at their work, the healers needed to be versed in the art of evil hexing caused by bad witches, so quite naturally their knowledge and experience necessarily included both spectrums of the Craft. The Nahuatl word that most accurately describes the practitioners in this book is *tetlachihuic*. However, it must be noted that the Aztec language of Nahuatl contains some forty different words that translate into various specialties of witches, sorcerers, and spiritual healers; such is the range and depth of their knowledge of the supernatural. The tetlachihuics can be described as women or men with supernatural abilities to either induce or cure illness; manipulate people's consciousness for either good or bad; alter or influence events and circumstances through incantations, prayers, rites, ceremonies, and use of amulets, talismans, and effigies; and who are skilled in the use of plants and animals.

The "master" witches I encountered in the Tuxtlas, and who ended up being my teachers, had all of the abilities of the tetlachihuic plus many more. Specifically, they are also specialists in what I'm going to describe as conscious dreaming, or dream trance. This is a state of consciousness that allows the witch to consciously "fly" into the realm of the spirit underworld and "bring back" into everyday life information on illness and curing especially having to do with soul loss or spirit possession. My teachers of witchcraft described in this book are so highly skilled at manipulating consciousness via the dream trance that they can even manipulate the dream trances of others. Throughout this book, you will have the opportunity to see exactly what I experienced and how I learned through their teachings.

In the beginning of my instruction, I was given various species of the datura plant to facilitate the dream-trance state. Once I had experienced the dream-trance state via the datura sufficiently to alter my "everyday," or normal, consciousness, the datura was no longer necessary, although it was still employed on some occasions during extreme circumstances.

The usage of datura leads to a deviation from practicality with this latest book. As expressed in my warning, I do not advise anyone to ingest datura. I was thrown into the world of datura without my consent, and I am lucky to be alive and relatively sane. Datura usage is included in this book simply because it was a major factor and central part of my lessons with this specific class of witches. However, the main crux of the knowledge shared with me by my teachers, and what I want to share with you, is the dream trance and positive applications of working with the spirits of the underworld. Witchcraft in the Tuxtlas is fundamentally about spirit possession and/or soul loss. It is not necessary to experience or work in the realms of spirits and souls with datura. That's just what happened to me when I went to Veracruz.

Practically speaking, I would make at least three separate contexts for spirit possession as I was introduced to it in the Tuxtlas. First and most rare are people afflicted involuntarily by a spirit. Second are those who voluntarily are possessed, such as witches, shamans, sorcerers, etc. Third are those possessed involuntarily by a spirit not acting entirely of its own volition but rather at the bidding of someone controlling it, such as a witch or shaman.

With soul loss, there are two main categories. First is involuntary soul loss through extreme personal events or the soul being taken by a witch or shaman. Second is voluntary soul loss by witches and shamans that sends their souls flying into other worlds.

The concepts and experiences of working with spirits and souls during the flight of the dream trance is the central form of witchcraft that I experienced with the witches of Catemaco and the Tuxtlas mountain region. Although many of the experiences I share here may be disturbing to some people, as they were to me, ultimately the healing knowledge acquired from these experiences is, I feel, worth the price and merits sharing.

And boy was it a wild ride...

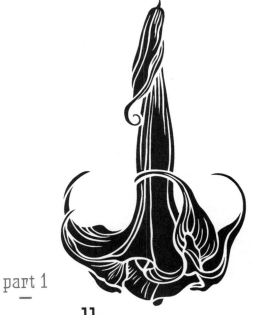

part 1

witches, spells, and consequences

what the bleep?

this is what I felt as I began to wake up: I was shivering on cold, hard ground. Slowly I got up on my hands and knees, but as I tried to look around, the pitch-black darkness was so complete that I thought I must have gone blind. It's not often one can see and experience a true state of total darkness. In addition to my thought that I might be blind, I was experiencing an incredible headache and severe stomach pains.

I felt around on the ground and slowly came to realize that I was kneeling on hard, compact soil, and at almost the same moment my sense of smell began to register. There was a rancid smell in the air, one that I was familiar with: rotting flesh.

"What are you doing here, devil?" a raspy voice said to me in Spanish from the darkness.

Panicked as I was from suddenly hearing the voice, I tried to scramble away from it, but within just a few feet, I hit my head hard on what felt like a rock wall. Suddenly hitting the wall like this felt like when you are not paying attention going down some stairs and you accidentally miss the bottom one, and your whole equilibrium is shot in a split second. But the worst part was that I hit the wall so hard that my jaw snapped together, and I bit my tongue.

I growled in frustration and felt my forehead with my right hand: wet blood. *Just great,* I thought. I turned my body so that I had my back against the wall and slowly stood up on shaky legs. The inability to see was definitely freaking me out, and I strained to hear anything that would give me a clue about where I was or who had just spoken to me.

"Who are you, and where am I?" I yelled into the darkness, with my arms outstretched in front of me for protection.

No answer. But with my wits slowly coming to me, I hurriedly searched my pockets. Unfortunately, they were empty, and I had no idea where my knapsack was that I always had with me. Realizing now that I was in a totally helpless situation and that there was definitely at least one other person nearby, I figured my best bet was to remain calm and see what would happen next, so I simply sat down on the ground with my back to the wall and wiped the blood from my face with my shirt. My head was pounding so hard I was almost glad to be in the dark, except for the fact that the darkness was totally preventing me from doing or even knowing anything about my situation. The only things I knew for sure were these: I was hurt, I couldn't see, it was cold, I was somewhere with a dirt floor and a hard stone wall, there was at least one person around me somewhere, and I had nothing except what I was wearing.

"I asked you a question, *diablo.* What are you doing here?"

The voice was like an eerie whisper from a ghost in a cheap horror movie, but in that moment it sent chills through me like I had never felt before. There was something malicious and evil in that voice, and strangely enough I couldn't even tell if it was male or female. That fact might have creeped me out even more than anything else about it. But I decided not to give it the satisfaction of an answer. For one thing, I wasn't a devil, and I obviously had no idea what I was doing there. My mind was a complete blank.

"Many people are outside waiting to hang you," the eerie voice said. "I can take you to them right now if you like."

This was getting to be too much. Since I felt no breeze and heard no sounds, I had already guessed that I was inside. But inside where? And who was outside waiting for me? And where was outside?

"Why would anyone want to hang me?" I asked, figuring that was even more important than where I was or how I got there.

"You are either an evil witch or a demon or something worse. You carry the sacred objects of a Huichol shaman and an Aztec curandero, but you sleep for days in a portal to the underworld. Did you kill those people whose things you carry and steal their power?"

"No! Those are all my things, and don't you touch them, or you will be sorry."

"Ha, ha, ha," the voice cackled in the darkness, and this time I heard a distinct echo, as if we were in a large space or maybe underground. "Why don't you run from me, diablo?"

"Run? I can't see a thing and can barely stand up. I have obviously been seriously injured. Why aren't you helping me? Why have you taken my things? From where I am sitting, *you* are the evil one."

Just then, a good-size stone hit me square in the chest, and the voice cackled even louder. Whoever it was had just thrown a stone at me. Oh, this was getting better by the minute!

"I guess you really can't see," the voice hissed. "Here, tie your ankles together tight—and no games, or I will stick you with my knife and make you squeal."

A short rope was thrown at me, and I tied my ankles.

"Now hold your arms out in front of you."

With lightning speed, my wrists were tied together, and the person moved away. I heard some movement, and then, as if out of nowhere, the single flame from a candle appeared on the ground right in front of me. But as excited as I felt about being able to see, something was still severely wrong. My vision was extremely blurry, like I was underwater with my eyes open and the water was moving and unclean. I tried to focus on the light and rubbed my eyes, but nothing helped. The light, the shadows, everything was blurry. The thought crossed my mind that I might have a severe concussion.

Surprisingly, now that I could sort of see the light and knew I wasn't completely blind, I began to feel even more frightened than before. It was as if when I was completely in the dark and feeling totally helpless, there was nothing I could do, but now that I knew I could see, I had to do something—but I had no idea what. The blurriness of my vision was making me feel even sicker, so I closed my eyes and took a few deep breaths, trying to clear my mind.

"How long have I been here?" I finally managed to ask. And it was in that moment I realized how incredibly thirsty I was. My throat, lips, and even eyes were so incredibly dry. I felt like I hadn't had anything to drink in days.

"Not sure, but at least three days and nights since the people first found you," a new voice said.

My eyes shot open, and in the blur I could make out a tall figure standing in front of me, holding a torch of fire. This person was definitely male and actually had a kind but very deep voice, with a tone that was typical of a man of authority in Mexican culture. Upon hearing his voice, a few vague memories began to come to me like shadows. I finally realized that my last memories were of Mexico, and that's probably where I still was.

"Can you help me?" I asked sheepishly. "Or do you want to hang me as well?"

The man turned and said, "You can go now, Marisol. I will take this from here."

The voice in the dark hissed, and I heard someone moving away. "Marisol," the man said in a condescending voice, "leave his bag, and make sure all his things are in it."

The voice hissed again, and I heard a loud thump on the ground near me as Marisol obviously was going to take my bag but then threw it back when the man caught her. I was starting to like this guy, but upon hearing the name Marisol, which was female, my mind felt like it had been struck by lightning. I knew that name was familiar, but I had no memory of why.

Holding my head and trying desperately to remember, I listened as the man continued, "No one in this village is going to hang you—that would draw too much attention—but you are in grave danger unless you convince me that you are not evil. What are you doing here, sleeping in this cave?"

"I don't know," I replied honestly. "I don't know where I am or how I got here. That's the truth."

"Your accent says you are from the United States. Your Spanish is good, but it is strange. Where did you learn to speak it?"

"Mostly with the Huichol, in the mountains."

"Yes, they speak a strange Spanish, because it is not their language. Spanish is not my language either. But I speak five languages; would you rather speak in English?"

"Sure."

"So you say you spent time with the Huichol—is that why you have those Huichol things in your bag?"

"Yes."

"And what about the other things—the sacred objects of the Aztec curandero and dreamer?"

"I have been trained as a curandero by a Mazatec master healer."

"If that is true, then why do you sleep in this cave? If you were a real curandero, you would know that this is not a safe place for you to sleep."

"I had no idea I was even in a cave until you just told me. I just woke up here a few minutes ago, and I am having trouble with my eyes."

"Tell me why it is not safe to sleep in this cave," the man demanded.

I knew right away by his question that he was going to test me to see if what I had been saying was true. Since I now knew I was in a cave and that it must be either very deep or long since there was no ambient light, and it reeked of rotting flesh that was most likely from animal or human sacrifices that were left to the lords of the underworld by local curanderos or brujos, it was likely I was in a sacred cave—a portal to the underworld.

"Some caves are portals to the underworld. If you sleep in them, you risk having your *tonal* taken or enslaved by an evil being while you are dreaming," I replied.

"What is your *nagual*?" he asked.

"Condor."

"Who rules the naguals?"

"The Lord of the Animals."

"What other entities are your allies?"

"Here or there?" I asked him back.

"Both," he countered knowingly.

"You know I can't tell you that."

"Look!" he said sharply. "I am trying to save you. I don't believe you are evil, but the news has spread like wildfire that there is a *gringo brujo* sleeping in this cave, and your life is in serious danger. I have already looked inside the sacred case you were carrying that houses your spirit allies. I have let no one else see it. If your tale is true, you will know exactly what the case contains and the meaning of each item; if you don't, that means you are a liar and a thief, and you will never make it out of these mountains alive. So start talking."

Easing myself up off the ground as best I could, I stood up straight and replied, "I am Condor and carry the Condor muvieri; my allies are the Blue Deer—I carry the sacred deer hide; the Eagle—I carry the eagle muvieri; the Cougar—I carry the cougar-teeth rattle; the King Snake—I carry his fifth skin; the Wolves of Datura—I carry their seed; Itzamna, Lord of Uxmal—I carry his sacred juice; and Matziwa the Traveler—I carry his *hikuri*."

Some of the items I mentioned and the names I used for them were also my little test of the man asking the questions. If he knew what he was talking about, he would be familiar with those terms and items.

"You have many powerful allies," the man said in his kind voice once again. "So tell me, now that you know you are in a deep cave, where would you say that you are exactly?"

Another test, but in terms of caves to the underworld, that was an easy question. The stench of flesh, the hissing voice of the woman Marisol, the fact that people were afraid of me sleeping in this cave, the complete darkness, the cold—all pointed to one place in this man's cosmology. "We are in the underworld entrance of the north, Mictlan, the Place of the Dead."

"Here is your bag," the deep-voiced man said as he threw my pack at me and extinguished his torch.

I quickly found my water bottle and chugged down the contents. Even in the dark, I could find anything in my pack. After traveling with it for many years, I knew it better than any lover.

"Tell me what you know of the soul, *gringo curandero.*"

Now we were getting right to it; his previous test questions were cursory at best for someone with my experience. Without using the word, he had already asked me about the soul, but now he was searching deeper. However, in quickly assessing my situation, I was in no mood to answer more questions. I just wanted to get the hell out of there and find out what in the world had happened to me. On the other hand, I still couldn't see properly, and I doubted if I could successfully escape from him or the cave. The only good part of the whole situation was that he referred to me as curandero, which meant he called me a healer, and not as a *brujo*, an evil witch, like the hissing voice of Marisol had accused me of being.

The concept of "soul" is very tricky even in casual conversation, and between the world's religions it can be a very hot topic. But when injured in a dark cave somewhere in Mexico and dealing with a man who obviously was some sort of priest or holy man sent to the cave of the underworld to question an American guy suspected of being a devil, the questioning could turn ugly real fast. I knew from experience that the soul was at the heart of indigenous beliefs, especially in Mexico, where the Aztecs were known for tearing out a person's heart to offer their soul to God. So I had to be very wary as to how to answer this somewhat simple question.

"May I ask your name?" I responded, unsure how to proceed under the circumstances.

"My name is Vicente. Now tell me about your soul, or I will kill you and leave your rotting corpse here among the other dead."

At this point, I actually almost laughed because I was so scared.

"I have three souls," I blurted out.

"Go on."

"You asked earlier about my tonal and nagual, but I prefer to use the ancient words."

"Go on."

"My *yolia* animates my body. My *tonalli* is my heat of life."

"Which came first?"

"The yolia comes at conception, the tonalli at birth."

"So what about the third one?"

"That's the one I'm going to kill you with if you don't stop asking me questions and show me the way out of this stinking place," I replied, trying to sound tough but not really feeling it.

"You have more than one *nagualli, gringo curandero.* Which will you summon to try and kill me?"

Loud and vicious growling suddenly filled the cave; my two spirit wolves had arrived. But Vicente merely laughed and cut me free from my bonds.

"My wolves are standing right next to you," I admonished him.

"Yes, they are quite beautiful, the wolves of Kieri," he replied knowingly.

Panic hit me once again, even stronger this time. Vicente had just used the name Kieri; I hadn't used it. If he could see my wolves and knew their name, he must be one of the most powerful and therefore most dangerous shamans I had ever met. My opinion of this man instantly changed, and from then on, I called him Don Vicente out of respect.

"The wolves of Kieri seem to be your allies," Don Vicente said as I could hear my wolves licking his face like that of an old friend, "but there is much for you yet to learn about the devil's weed—the datura, or *Kieri,* as it is sometimes called.

These wolves of Kieri that you have are not from the devil, and you are not an evil witch, so maybe we should just go and have some lunch."

———

catemaco

U nder the care of Don Vicente, who turned out to be one of the most respected curanderos (shaman/healers) of the area, I gradually regained my health and most of my memories. During many days and nights, Don Vicente probed my mind, and in doing so, he finally concluded that I had indeed been trained by many medicine teachers, including the Huichol and Mazatec. Throughout the days, and with the help of an unexpected guest, I was able to piece together the events that led to me sleeping in the cave where the people found me.

I had originally come to Mexico a few weeks before to participate in a Huichol ceremony being held up in one of the most remote Huichol villages in the Western Sierra Madres. The invitation had come from my longtime Huichol friend Alberto many months before, but in the weeks leading up to my trip, I was unsuccessful in contacting him. When I arrived in Mexico City and called the satellite phone in Nueva Colonia, which is the closest phone to the village of Santa Catarina, where the ceremony was to be held, I was told that the three-day ceremony had already been completed. This wasn't the greatest news for me, but I wasn't very surprised. The Huichol shamans don't base what they do on our Gregorian calendar. They operate in conjunction with the wet and dry seasons and the planting and harvesting of their crops. Some ceremonies are also conducted in accordance with the head shaman's dreams, so it's difficult to accurately predict when a certain ceremony will be held.

I still could have visited my friends in the Huichol Sierras, but in staying with my *chilango* (Mexico City) friends, I heard them talking about going on a weekend trip to Veracruz. Every year on the first Thursday of March the *Congreso Internacional de Brujería* (the International Conference of Witchcraft) begins in the "witch capital of Mexico," Catemaco. Having stayed previously for a few weeks in coastal Veracruz City, I already knew about the popular "witch" trade in that part of the country, but checking out the International Conference of Witchcraft sounded way too interesting to pass up. Plus, we were able to get a cheap overnight bus directly to Catemaco.

Catemaco is an astounding place, and it's no wonder that the area is known for its mystical energy and power. The volcanic Los Tuxtlas Mountains that dominate the region are often referred to as a geologic anomaly disconnecting the region from the massive central Mexican plateau. The spectacular geographic features of the region range from mist-shrouded dormant and extinct volcanoes to coastal sand dunes, placid lagoons, and roaring waterfalls. The city of Catemaco sits aside the twenty-eight-square-mile Lake Catemaco, which is abundant in fish and small volcanic islands that are home to scads of macaque monkeys. However, as idyllic as Catemaco would seem in a travel brochure, it becomes painfully obvious what life is really like there once you begin to explore the outskirts of the city. The roads are in shambles, the economy is stagnant, and over half of the people receive federal, state, and local subsidies to survive. This is "rustic" Mexico at its best—or worst—and has none of the glamour of popular tourist destinations such as Cancún or Acapulco.

But during the annual witch conference, the city of Catemaco was bustling with people and filled to the brim with life and activity. The majority of the visitors are Mexicans from all over the country, and the city is so full that people even sleep in their cars. Our small group was able to find a room to keep our stuff in and to use the bathroom, but it was barely large enough to sleep in. One of my chilango friends, Marisol, had grown up in Veracruz City and was very familiar with the witch scene and Catemaco. Over the course of our first day, Marisol became our tour guide, and with her extremely outgoing personality and knowledge of Catemaco history, we blended in extremely well with the controlled chaos of the festival.

For lunch, Marisol took us to a street vendor whom she had apparently known for years and who was famous for his tegogolo cocktail, which is a mixture of snails from Lake Catemaco and a strong red sauce similar to how Mexicans typically eat shrimp. Marisol humorously declined the dish for herself, stating that locals believe the tegogolo to be stronger than Viagra, so she would leave us men to it. But after the tegogolo we were still hungry, so we sampled another Catemaco street delicacy, rabbit, as Marisol gave us a brief history of Catemaco, which revealed that the Tuxtlas's mountainous area had remained fairly isolated from the outside world all the way up until the twentieth century. The oldest Mexican civilization, the Olmecs, had inhabited this region since somewhere around 3000 BC. Isolation and such ancient roots are two of the main reasons that brujería (witchcraft, sorcery, shamanism) is said to have survived in this area more than other regions. The first train tracks didn't arrive in the area until 1912, and it wasn't until the 1950s that the first paved roads entered the region. This relative isolation, coupled with the enormous quantity of medicinal plants that have their home in the tropical jungles around Catemaco, have very naturally kept the native peoples reliant on traditional folk medicines and curanderos (healers) rather than on modern medical practices and treatments.

Marisol also had some knowledge of the modern history of Catemaco brujería and was an excellent storyteller. With waves of people flocking by the crowded, sunny streets, she had us totally captivated by her stories at our tiny outdoor table, sucking on rabbit bones. According to local legend, the founder of Congreso Internacional de Brujería, Gonzalo Aguirre Pech, had sold his soul to the devil just before he cast an evil spell that killed his boss, who was the head brujo of the region. The huge success of Gonzalo during the following years seemed to confirm the speculation of him selling his soul. Some of the stories about Gonzalo include consultation visits from Mexican presidents and politicians, famous movie stars, and other wealthy clients, and that if someone would cross him, he would turn them into a rat or some other small creature and then nail them on the door outside his office for all to see.

Now that we were really getting into the topic of witches, it was obvious that Marisol was in her element. After she jokingly asked us guys how we felt in our pants after the stimulating snails, she proceeded to inform us that not only was the "witch" Gonzalo extremely successful, but so were his offspring and his apprentices. With an air of mysteriousness, she added that she knew one of the heads of the current Catemaco brujería and that she could take us to see him.

At the time, I didn't really see what the big deal was about meeting the guy. Even though the city was currently thriving on the witches' conference, I imagined that in a small city like Catemaco even a prestigious leader couldn't be hard to find. But I was wrong. Strolling through the packed streets of Catemaco, there were witches of every kind imaginable selling their trade in stalls along the streets or out of busses and vans, and of course the Catemaco native witches were working out of their homes. Most of the witches were selling *limpias*, cleansings of the energy field, for 50 to 100 pesos (4 to 9 dollars). Other specialties included fortunetelling, massages, and the making of all kinds of magic potions and amulets.

Beneath the often cheesy tourist scams (some "witches" were highly entertaining) was a much darker world in Catemaco that is scarcely noticed by the common visitor. Much to my dismay, I would find this out firsthand. Maybe because the festive atmosphere of the witches' conference left my guard down to anything sinister, or possibly due to the fact that the first "real" witch I encountered, the one whom Marisol introduced us to, was completely not what I expected.

Don Julio had a lavish office and residence overlooking the lake. He was actually a licensed medical doctor, and he took my surprise at seeing his diplomas hanging on the wall behind his desk in stride. Throughout our conversation, Don Julio made it quite clear that he had extensive knowledge of "black" magic, learned primarily from the former head witch Gonzalo, of whom he had been an apprentice for many years. But mostly he was now simply a healer.

"Back then we used to make lots of money," Don Julio said. "Politicians would come and sell their souls so that one of their competitors would die. Or sometimes people would come for potions to kill an enemy or someone that they owed money to, or to bewitch a cheating spouse. We would charge thousands of dollars for those services." From the looks of his surroundings and the intense manner with which he spoke, I didn't doubt him one bit. But he didn't offer us any "evil" services. His claim was that he simply gave people what they needed. "Good witches provide a valuable social service; most people around here can't pay for proper medical treatment, or it is simply not available to them.

"People in these mountains believe in witchcraft, so that is what I give them to keep them healthy and happy. Also, being a man of science, I sometimes have to trick my patients by giving them a pharmaceutical medicine but telling them it's a magical potion. Am I really lying? Basically, I am part witch doctor, part medical doctor, and part psychologist. If a woman comes to me hysterical about her husband running away with another woman, I give her medicine to calm her down and a charm to convince her that he will come back. If someone comes with a broken bone, I set it, rub it with a 'magical' ointment, and cast it. Simple!"

We were then interrupted by the doorbell, and Don Julio explained that he had a meeting scheduled. Leaving his office and walking toward the front gate, I couldn't help but feel slightly duped by the whole witches' conference. But just as I opened the gate, I happened to look down—and there, on the ground, was an old human skull. In that same moment, shocked as I was, I didn't notice someone else coming through the gate, and I ran smack into him. That's when I first met Don Julio's son, Rafael.

After apologies, it became apparent that Marisol knew Rafael, and that Rafael wanted to know Marisol better. The strikingly handsome and well-dressed Rafael immediately guessed correctly that his father hadn't provided what we were looking or hoping for, so he invited us to join him in a "real" brujo ceremony that night and gave Marisol the directions. As we left, I couldn't get that skull out of my mind. Marisol quickly brushed it off, saying that "lots of witches have bones lying around, it is part of the show." But, as I turned to get one more view of the house, Don Julio was in the upstairs window, staring down at me while his son was speaking rapidly to him and waving his arms about. If I had known better, I would have seen the evil eye of Rafael.

———

rafael

M arisol quickly said, "I don't know a whole lot about Don Julio, but Rafael organizes a lot of the witches' conference, and he's the one I really wanted you to meet. People say he is a powerful witch even though he is still young. They call him the shapeshifter, because he can turn himself into various animals and birds or he can be seen at two places at the same time."

This sounded much more like what I had hoped for, although I secretly wished that Rafael had been a woman. He obviously had a thing for Marisol, and the more I got to know her, the more I was enamored of her as well. Oh, well; a little competition was always fun—besides, I was really there to learn more about the witches of Catemaco, and Rafael did seem to fit the bill.

We arrived at his place just before sunset. It was just as gorgeous as his father's, albeit half the size. Rafael was a superior host: jovial, accommodating, intelligent, and gracious. Definitely a consummate lady's man, he openly yet in a most clandestine manner succeeded in flirting with Marisol while keeping the rest of us entertained with his personal stories and some obscure legends of Catemaco and the surrounding mountains and villages. Marisol could not take her eyes off him. Not knowing how long of a night we were in for and what kind of ceremony there would be, I had brought my small backpack with a few extra clothes, some water, and my *takwatsi* (case with my sacred objects/allies), which Rafael glanced at more than once when he thought I wasn't looking. This, more than anything else, alerted me to the fact that at least on some level Rafael was probably the real deal and could feel the power of the sacred items hidden in my pack.

Rafael served us some fabulous margaritas made with the juice of fresh prickly pear cactus and a huge plate of steaming empanadas. Everyone was having a great time, and I was glad I had decided to visit Catemaco. Around ten o' clock, Rafael said we should head down to the beach for the ceremony.

We walked along the beach for a half hour or so to a secluded area where about thirty people were gathered around a large fire. Rafael was greeted by a swarm of people, and he introduced us to some of them. But for some reason, I was suddenly feeling overwhelmed and very sleepy, and I told my friends I was going to go sit down away from the crowd for a while. Just outside the light of the fire and the crowd of people, I found a nice place to sit and view the fire, the people, the water, and the sky.

Surprisingly, a few moments later my spirit wolves appeared, and each lay down on either side of me as if waiting for something. I lovingly stroked the top of their heads and ears but I was also curious as to what they were doing. Normally, my spirit wolves came to me in very special or distressful moments, or during my dream journeys to the underworld. I first acquired my spirit wolves as allies many years before while I was living with the Huichol. On that occasion, a very angry and jealous young Huichol man who thought of me as a threat had poisoned me by blowing the dust of the devil's weed (*Datura inoxia*) into my eyes. I was unconscious for three days, and during that time I was transformed into a young wolf by the visions of the devil's weed, also known to the Huichol as Kieri. In my visions, the two wolves—one black and the other white—were my parents; they taught me about being a wolf. Before waking from my visions, I saved my parents' lives from hunters looking to kill them, and when I finally awoke, the two wolves from the spirit realm followed me and have been my guardians and allies ever since. So my first and only encounter with the devil's weed turned out to be a blessing rather than the usual outcomes of ingesting it, which can include paranoid schizophrenia, different types of permanent psychosis, or even death.

With these memories and thoughts rolling through my mind, I began to realize that my eyesight was getting blurry, and I knew something was very wrong. In that moment, another spirit ally, Itzamna, appeared in front of me. Itzamna is the dwarf king of the ancient city of Uxmal in the Yucatan, and he has been my ally ever since I drank the sacred secretions of the magical toads and met him at the Pyramid of the Magician at Uxmal years before. As far as spirit allies go, Itzamna is in a class of his own. A funny but extremely powerful little dwarf, he is one of my most interesting and entertaining allies.

The usually cheerful and carefree Itzamna did not look happy as he silently stared at me. My wolves got up to greet him, and as he petted them, Itzamna looked over to the crowd gathered around the fire and said, "You've been witched, you silly fool."

He threw his hands into the air, and all at once I was in my condor body, flying over the water. The condor is my animal counterpart in the underworld—my alter ego in altered states of consciousness that I use to explore other realities. This time I was in trouble and needed all the help I could get. I flew high over the crowd of people at the fire, and as I circled I saw for the first time that there were some spirit animals in the crowd as well. Most of them were around Rafael and Marisol. Now I knew for sure that Rafael was a curandero or a brujo, and to my surprise, so was Marisol.

I circled around and dropped lower for a closer look, but Rafael suddenly saw me, and with lightning speed he pulled a hair out of his long black mane. As I watched, it magically turned into an arrow, which he then shot right at me.

Wounded and whimpering, I landed back into my body, sitting on the rock. "That evil witch Rafael poisoned you with the devil's weed and now he has shot you with a wicked dart. What is it with you and the devil's weed, my friend?" Itzamna asked calmly but with a concerned look.

"I don't know," I replied. "I did nothing to Rafael. I thought we were friends."

"He is an evil *brujo*, an evil witch—you cannot be friends with someone like that. All he wants is power. He is threatened by your presence here and will do whatever it takes to be rid of you. Did you eat or drink with him?"

"Yes," I replied, and in a flash I knew what Rafael had done. I thought it was a little strange at the time but I didn't take much notice of it: Rafael's prickly pear margaritas had the seeds of the prickly pear fruit in them, which is no big deal even though most people usually strain them out, but in this case he used the prickly pear seeds to hide the seeds of the devil's weed in my drink. I didn't even notice the difference. It was an ingenious way of poisoning me.

Rafael's dart, which had hit me in the side, really ached, but more importantly I could feel the full effects of the devil's weed beginning to overwhelm me, and I knew that I would soon lose consciousness.

Involuntarily closing my eyes, I fell off the rock and landed on my side on the ground. "I can't help you much with this," Itzamna said. "The wolves and I can protect you from other spirits that may want to attack you, but we have little power in the physical world. I will talk with your friend Marisol since she is obviously a skilled witch, and I don't think she is evil. If she is not, I will ask her to look after your physical body."

That's the last thing I remember about being conscious before I passed out.

marisol

"So I guess you're not a devil after all," I heard the chilling voice from the cave hiss at me from behind. Startled, I jumped up and stood facing the voice. I could not possibly have been more surprised. It was Marisol.

Don Vicente laughed out loud at the expression on my face as I tried to grasp what was happening. It was the first day after Don Vicente had brought me to his house after rescuing me from the cave, and we were sitting in the shade of the patio in the back of his house and talking quietly.

Seeing how utterly perplexed I was, Marisol gave me a hug and then pulled up a chair and sat down with us around the small table. A million questions were running through my mind, but I was still foggy from everything that happened and couldn't even formulate into words what I wanted to know. Thankfully, Don Vicente began. "James, Marisol is my daughter, and she is in training to be a curandera."

His daughter!

"Marisol, why didn't you tell me?" I asked.

"You did not need to know. Plus, I figured if you were to find out, it would be in the proper time and context. The doings of curanderos and brujos in this part of the world are full of secrets and events that happen behind the scenes of normal reality. I didn't know Rafael had become so evil. I would never intentionally put you in danger like that. I apologize for my lack of sight. I guess I was blind to his real essence because I wanted him to be something different, more like his father. He not only fooled you, he fooled me even worse, because I thought I knew him."

I felt bad for Marisol, because it wasn't her fault what had happened. But then I remembered that evil hissing voice from the cave that she had just used again.

"Was that really you in the cave where I woke up? Your hissing voice sounded like a demon or something worse. How could that possibly have been you?"

Don Vicente laughed again as I stared at Marisol in disbelief.

"You have to understand, James," Marisol explained. "We weren't sure what had happened to you except that it was obvious that the James I knew had been witched. What we didn't know—and needed to find out—was to what extent you had been witched, the type of witchcraft used on you, and if you were still really James and not some evil spirit from the underworld inhabiting your body. Since you had flown to the cave of the underworld, we suspected the worst and had to deal with you as though you were a malevolent spirit until we could prove one way or the other who you really were. One of my gifts is the use of my voice and my body. My father has been teaching me to use my gifts since I was a small child, and so I am highly skilled at sounding or appearing as something different than I normally am."

My head was spinning with all this new information, and even though I was beginning to piece together what had happened to me, I was still confused about many things, primarily what had happened after I passed out on the beach and how I got to the cave of the dead, which was far into the mountains. Since Marisol was there on the beach with me that night, I asked her about it.

"Well, first of all," Marisol began, "I had no idea you were in trouble until your little dwarf friend jumped out from the fire and scolded me for not looking after you. Itzamna pulled me away from Rafael and the crowd and explained to me what was going on. During our conversation, he realized the extent of my training in brujería and curanderismo and advised me to get away from Rafael and to go help you. From that point, he didn't need to state the obvious—that I let my infatuation with Rafael cloud my perception, and as a result, you had been witched without me even knowing. I'm sorry, James."

Marisol took her eyes from me and with a bowed head stared at the ground as if awaiting some sort of punishment. I looked to Don Vicente, not knowing what to do. I certainly had no ill feelings toward Marisol in any way.

Don Vicente leaned over, gently raised his daughter's chin with his hand, and said, "This has been a big lesson for both of you. Neither of you are to blame. This experience will only serve to make you stronger and wiser. Now, Marisol, tell James what he needs to know."

Marisol carefully lit a beautiful votive candle that was sitting in the middle of the table, and as she stared into the flame, she began her story in yet another voice that I hadn't heard before.

"By the time Itzamna and I were done talking and we went back to where you were sitting on the beach, you were already gone. I was in total panic, but Itzamna lent me his vision, and I saw where you went. You had flown to an affluent neighborhood about a mile away and were jumping in and out of an empty swimming pool in the back of a vacant house. When I arrived, you paid no attention to me and continued to jump feet-first into the deep end of the pool and then climb out and do it again. This went on for about two hours until you went onto the diving board and were jumping really high, and it looked like you were going to dive head-first into the empty pool. But right at the last second a giant eagle came"—this was Ronnie, one of my spirit guides—"and pulled you off the board before you jumped.

"After that, you went into convulsions and then lay as if dead for quite a while. But death didn't take you, and you began to speak in various languages as if possessed. Finally standing up again, you raised your arms and began pacing back and forth while screaming at the devil and at God. You shouted at them to show themselves if they truly existed—to prove that they existed. You yelled at them repeatedly to show you their power, and when they didn't, you cursed at them and called them figments of imagination. You dared them to strike you down. You called them names and challenged them to demonstrate their power.

"Then you went to a cemetery and spoke with the dead. You asked them many questions, but none of them could give you the answer you were looking for because those spirits had not yet completely left this world and did not possess the knowledge you were seeking about death, God, and the devil.

"You went to Rafael's house, but he pretended not to be home. He was alone and did not want to see you, but you busted a window and climbed into his house. It was dark and he tried to sneak up on you and probably kill you with a knife, but your wolves were with you and he had no chance. Your wolves were acting as crazy as you were, and so Rafael's animal allies were scared and ran away. You and your wolves forced Rafael to serve you drinks and sit and answer questions. For more than an hour you picked Rafael's brain with questions about death, afterlife, and why he had poisoned you. During that whole time you drank enough tequila to kill a person, but you didn't act drunk at all. That scared Rafael even more. When you finally got bored with him and told him he didn't really know anything, you promised him that his evil deed would not go unpunished but that it would not be by your hand. And then you left through the front door, with Rafael cowering on the floor.

"You started walking out of the city, and when you finally came to the jungle, you sat down at the base of a large tree. Incredibly, the whole time you were walking through the city, no one, including the police, even seemed to notice you. It was then that I knew you were truly flying in the spirit world and were virtually invisible to people who don't see spirits. I sat with you under the tree, but you took no notice of me and began talking to the tree. Eventually you stood up, facing the tree, and while hugging it you asked for forgiveness for all your sins. You asked the spirit of the tree to help you be cleansed and to show you the true reality of life and death. Begging and crying, you climbed to the top of the tree and out of my sight. When all became quiet, I climbed up the tree, but you were gone. The only thing I found was a condor feather."

Marisol continued looking into the flame for a few moments in silence and then looked toward her father.

Don Vicente began, "Marisol came to me and told me the whole story and gave me the feather. I went into my dreaming and found you in the underworld. I found your double, which is the condor, flying above the cave of the dead, and that's when I knew where you were. By the time Marisol and I went up into the mountains, some people had already seen you lying in the cave, and word had spread that a gringo devil had emerged from the cave of the dead. When we got to the cave, I chased all the people away and examined you. You were in a catatonic state, and Marisol and I took turns watching you for two days until you woke up. I instructed Marisol to be extremely careful if you woke up because we had no idea if your soul would survive or if it had been taken and replaced by something else.

"The fact that you have actually survived the attack of the witch Rafael has given me much thought, and I have concluded that you were brought to us for a special reason. I have been waiting for a sign that would bring to me my apprentice to share my knowledge and continue my healing work. As hard as it is for me to fathom, I believe the spirits have chosen you. We will begin with your teachings right away. You are now a part of a very small community of powerful witches. Your apprenticeship here will be the most difficult thing you have ever experienced. But the spirits have delivered you to us, and now your path has been set."

———

los brujos pequeños

there are many different kinds of witches, both good and evil, male and female, in these Tuxtlas Mountains that are the ancient home of the Olmecs," Don Vicente began as we sat on a couch after Marisol left us with a look on her face that showed she was extremely concerned at her father's decision to teach me, because she knew the dangers.

"The Olmecs that lived here were before the Mexica (Aztec), or Maya, or anyone else. Their ways extend back into time immemorial, although throughout the centuries many things have been forgotten and many things added; such is the way of life and civilizations. You are already familiar with many of the practices of the good witches, which in Spanish we call *curanderos*, healers. But throughout the world and especially here, where the Mexican civilizations were born, we also have many evil witches, *brujos*, and now you must learn about them too, because it seems you have been chosen to go into combat with them.

"Some of what I am going to teach you are secrets, and some is common knowledge for people who do these kinds of things. You may share with whomever you like the teachings that are not secret, but some things you should never tell or show anyone. These secret teachings are passed down from one curandero to another, and that is all—unless the pupil dies, and then the instructor can teach someone else. You must teach the secret practices to someone of your choosing someday, just as I am going to teach them to you. Although I am teaching my daughter many things, she is learning the secret practices from a female curandera. This is part of the rule and cannot be broken. Don Julio is passing his knowledge to his son Rafael, but Rafael is still very inexperienced compared to his father, just as you are inexperienced compared to me. Rafael is still in the lower class of brujos, what we will call *los brujos pequeños* (little witches). But that is not because he has a bad teacher. Don Julio is one of the most powerful curanderos and brujos in the world. Don't let the fact that he is a highly educated medical doctor fool you—he is also a witch of the highest class. But his son lacks discipline and courage. To attack you the way he did was coward's work. I'm sure Don Julio will punish him for his cowardly actions."

"Why do you call Don Julio both a curandero and a brujo?"

"Almost everyone here in the Tuxtlas knows some curing and some evil witching. But in terms of evil, there are three types of professional brujos. You must know some about the magic of all three brujos even though you are a curandero like

Don Julio and myself. If you did not know about brujería, you could not heal people who are harmed by brujos. For a curand-ero, discipline involves learning and using brujería just enough to be able to cure it but not enough to be seduced by it."

Don Vicente got up from his chair and headed toward his large oak bar. "Let's have a drink and talk casually about these things on this beautiful sunny day," he said while pouring two small glasses of some type of strong liquor, which I guessed was pulque. He brought the drinks out onto the shaded veranda and asked if I would like a smoke with him. Knowing that it is cus-tomary, I accepted, and he lit my cigarette and then his as we sat in comfortable chairs overlooking his garden.

"You have not been around many brujos, have you?" Don Vicente asked.

"No, not many," I replied, just as a wave of euphoria blew through my mind.

"You must be more careful, James; brujos can kill you with an innocent little cigarette offered in a most kind and relaxed manner."

Euphoria was suddenly replaced with panic as I hurriedly put out the cigarette.

"Don't worry, James," Don Vicente added in a fatherly tone. "This is just a lesson for you to be on your guard. What I gave you was a small dose of a healing herb hidden in that cigarette. Sit back and relax and enjoy it—you need to learn about its soul. But realize that you never accept anything from a brujo unless he takes some first. It doesn't matter if it's a drink or a smoke or your favorite food. In this case, what you should have done was very politely asked me to do the honors of lighting the cigarettes so that you could have chosen your own from the pack. If I did not agree, then you would know that I was trying to witch you. Even if I did agree, that still would not prove I wasn't trying to witch you, but at least you wouldn't have gotten witched. Any brujo worth his salt would know right away about you if you asked to choose and light the cigarette. It is expected in this case of two brujos talking even if they are friends. From now on, when you are in areas like this that are full of witches, you must be on your guard all the time. I have taken you as my apprentice, so I will not intentionally harm you, but plenty of others could try at any moment, just like Rafael did."

The smoke potion was actually very nice. I felt comfortable, relaxed, and somewhat carefree. Under the influence of the smoke, I couldn't really imagine anyone wanting to hurt me, even though I knew Don Vicente was being dead serious.

"So am I to live in fear now, Don Vicente? Afraid to eat or drink or smoke?"

"No. What you need to do is be smarter, more alert, and raise your perception of what is going on around you to a higher level than that of those who might attack you. A good curandero can see or feel an attack by a brujo pequeno a mile away. Plus, I will also teach you how to make some protective items in case a more experienced brujo attacks you.

"What you have just smoked is a tiny bit of *coaxihuitl,* or what some people call the plant of the Virgin Mary (a type of morning glory). We use this smoke to help cure people when they are witched by brujos pequeños who use plant mixtures that are given to the victim through food, drink, smoke, kissing, or any other type of physical contact. This is what brujos pequeños do—they poison people to make them fall in love, to take advantage of them sexually, or to give them bad luck, especially with money, their business or profession, or with gambling. There are, of course, other antidotes, but this is a good one for you to start with because it works very well to break spells and to calm a victim down when they get distraught or angry from the witching. We use the coaxihuitl as a mild antidote because brujos pequeños don't kill with spells, but they can certainly do great harm. For more powerful brujos, we have to use more powerful remedies and protection."

———

los brujos negros

It was a hot day, and Don Vicente said we had a long walk ahead of us, but he didn't bother to tell me where we were going. He had me bring water and some fruit in my small pack to carry along with us. As is typical in the Tuxtlas, it began to rain, and searching for my hat, I simply could not find it in my pack, even though I was sure I had packed it.

"You can use mine," Don Vicente said while handing me his hat. "I have this nice light poncho with a hood that Marisol made for me," he said with a proud look as he took it out of his pack and put it on.

We walked for what must have been four to five hours through the dense jungle when Don Vicente stopped suddenly and, without ceremony, announced, "We are here," and took off his pack. I looked around the jungle and saw nothing much different from the terrain we had been walking in all day. I had no idea what was so special about this place; I figured we'd be going to someplace unique like a cave, a spring, or the top of a volcano.

Noticing me looking around skeptically, Don Vicente commented, "You didn't think my ancestors would lay their bodies back into the sacred mother in an obvious place where other people could easily find them, did you?"

Pondering his comment and the use of his words, I realized that we must be near a gravesite or cemetery. "Climb a little way up this tree here and look around," he instructed.

Upon careful inspection, it was clear that there were several places around us that were slightly raised like small mounds but were almost completely imperceptible from all of the jungle growth or from the ground. I would have walked right by them if I hadn't been in the tree overlooking the site.

"This is where you will learn about the *brujos negros*, the black witches, the second most powerful types of brujos."

Don Vicente had me help him clear a small area of brush with our machetes and get ready some wood for a small fire we would make when it got dark in a little while. With that done, he sat down with his back to a tree and relaxed. "It's going to be a long night, so I suggest you do the same," he said cryptically with a jut of his chin to a tree near him.

We sat in silence until the time was right, which was just before sunset. From his pack, Don Vicente brought out a small urn of the same type that is typically used to hold the ashes of a cremated person. "This I will transform into you," he announced, holding up the urn and then placing it on the ground in front of him.

"One thing that makes brujos negros so dangerous is that they never have to see or even meet you in order to witch you. They can cast a spell from any distance. All they need is a personal item of their victim, and anyone can bring it to them. Anything like clothing or jewelry will work, but the most potent spells are made with the victim's hair, nails, blood, urine, skin, or feces. Unlike brujos de muerte, the most evil and dangerous witches, the brujo negro's main intent is not to kill but to severely injure the victim or victims. Spells can be cast on people, animals, crops, or other objects such as tools or even vehicles. This is different from the brujo pequeno that is mostly interested in sex, love, wealth, or power. The brujo negro intends to do serious injury through extreme pain and suffering. That is why the spell needs such powerful things like pieces of the victim and the spell to be created in a place of the dead."

Don Vicente began to tell me that his teachers and their teachers for many generations were buried all around us, and that someday his body would be buried there too. While he was explaining this, he took out a glass container about the size of a Mason jar from his pack and dumped the dark-colored liquid contents into the urn. Then he slyly asked me for his hat back that he had lent me (right then I knew the old witch had taken mine from my pack so that I would wear his), and he very carefully pulled out some hairs from the straw and examined them. "These must be yours, James; they are much too long to be mine." And with that, he placed them into the urn and, with a straight stick he found on the ground, he mixed up the urn's contents.

"With your urine and feces that I collected from my outhouse without you knowing, and now some of your hair, I have a pretty strong brew of you that will affect your kidneys, intestines, penis, anus, and your head."

Don Vicente's previous admonishment of me to be careful when dealing with brujos was starting to finally sink into my thick skull. I had no idea that this eloquent, charming, and upstanding man could be so sneaky and vile. He was respected as one of the few master healers who still held to the old traditions, but to my amazement, he was obviously a skilled brujo as well, and I wondered how deep his knowledge of the dark arts went. Even though he claimed he would never intentionally harm me, I began to seriously wonder what his definition of "harm" really was. I was never so afraid of anyone in my life.

"There are two parts left to this incantation; these are the secret aspects that you are never to repeat until you are ready to pass your knowledge on to one apprentice. There are two sacred chants: one is sung before the urn is buried in the graveyard, and the other is sung after the urn is buried next to the dead. I will sing them both now."

"But wait! Don Vicente," I implored, "what is going to happen to me?"

"You are going to experience the witching of the brujo negro, but you will probably not die, and with the aid of your ally the devil's weed, I hope that you will come back with the anecdote and protection for this serious spell."

"But why do we have to do this in a graveyard? I have never spent a night in a graveyard in my life!"

"This is not just any graveyard," the old curandero/brujo rebuked me. "In this most holy ground are the remains of our teachers, and no matter what they do to you, they, like me, will not intentionally kill or seriously harm you. But the brujo negro spell works the best when performed in a graveyard, so that's where you should experience it. If I wanted to harm you, I would have taken this urn with your essences to a graveyard of some of those wicked brujo negros and buried it with them instead…"

Don Vicente began his complex chants, which I have recorded but will not repeat. When he was finished burying my urn in the graveyard and had sung his final chant, the sunlight was long gone and the fire we made had burnt down to cinders. The old brujo gave me a jar of the devil's weed brew and watched me drink the whole jar. When I asked him why I needed it, he simply said, "You may feel fine, but you are not fine. You have been poisoned, and the poison is the only thing that can cure you now." He then abruptly walked away, saying "*tengas buen viaje* (have a nice trip)" as he slipped into the darkness.

Watching Don Vicente disappear into the darkness of the jungle, I became mortally afraid for both my life and my soul. Not only were there many predatory and nocturnal animals in the jungle, but Don Vicente had just performed one of the most complex and disturbing rituals I had ever seen, and it had been conducted for the sole purpose of witching me so I could experience the evilness of the brujos negros. On top of all that, I had also just ingested a large quantity of a potent concoction of *Datura inoxia* that I knew would soon render me physically and mentally incapable of dealing with the tangible or ratio-nal world. If Don Vicente had actually left the area, which I assumed he did, I stood a high chance of being attacked, bitten, or even eaten by any number of jungle creatures, not to mention what ingesting the devil's weed would conjure up for me while in the graveyard of Don Vicente's brujo masters.

———

I came to my senses three days later. According to Don Vicente, I was crying hysterically and covered in blood, holding the guts of a monkey that lay dead next to me. After splashing water on me and calming me down enough to talk, Don Vicente imme-diately told me to close my eyes and recount my visions.

The first thing I remember was building the fire back up and collecting as much wood as I could find in the darkness to keep it going. By the time I was done collecting wood and had my fire going strong again, I really began to feel the effects of the devil's weed. My eyes began to blur, and the familiar feeling of an unquenchable thirst rapidly hit me.

Then, thankfully, my spirit allies came. First were my wolves, who snuggled close to me on both sides; they were tense and ready to spring, the hair standing up on their backs. They weren't happy that we were in the ancient graveyard. But the blue deer was calm, as if nothing could affect her. Ronnie the eagle landed in the tree above me, and when he did I caught a vision of what he was seeing as he surveyed the scene from above. For a little while I sat with him up there. I was in my condor body now, the lord of the sky. From a distance, I could see a movement in the bushes, and I knew my cougar had come.

He lay under the tree and yawned like the confident ally that he was. He knew there was nothing in that jungle that could harm him. But my snake was agitated, slithering back and forth as if a mongoose or something worse was near. Itzamna finally appeared down below me, and with a motion from his hands, he called me down to him.

"Are you strong enough to be here?" Itzamna asked with seeming trepidation.

I really wasn't sure what to say, and he knew it. Being in an unfamiliar dark jungle graveyard of a bunch of ancient curanderos and brujos and starting to begin my trip with the devil's weed was both better and scarier than any book I had ever read or story I had ever heard.

"You have two choices," Itzamna said. "You can continue with the visions of the devil's weed and learn why you are here. But your only allies will be the wolves of Kieri, and it will be a grueling test. Or you can simply lie down and sleep and be protected by all your allies as you sleep."

The little but powerful and ancient dwarf king stuck his hands in his pockets as if impatiently awaiting my decision. The comical part was that he knew what I would do, and he knew that I knew that he knew. It's a pretty hilarious situation to have that all running through your mind when you're tripping on devil's weed.

"I will stay and learn what Don Vicente brought me here for."

"So be it," the dwarf king replied. And in that moment, everything changed.

All of a sudden the lights came on: lights from above and all around. Multicolored lights moving to and fro like at a rock concert. And just like a rock concert, the music started, and it was so loud I felt like I was in the front row—which, ultimately, I was.

Walking, jumping, flipping, and spinning, a whole troupe of monkeys came out of the darkness. Leading the group was a very handsome-looking monkey, obviously the star of the show.

Grabbing his extra-large penis, he began stroking it to the rhythm of the music, and to my utter surprise I recognized the music as a Nine Inch Nails song. I looked over to Itzamna, but he was gone. In the distance I heard Itzamna yell, "HE IS THE EXIT!"

I had no clue what Itzamna meant, but by that time I was so mesmerized I didn't take too much notice. The dancing monkey rock concert was amazing. My only real trepidation was that like Itzamna had said, all my allies were also gone, except for my wolves, who were intricately tied to the devil's weed.

The lead monkey began singing in the multicolored light show, and the other monkeys provided the chorus. Taking a giant leap, the monkey singer landed right in front of me, so close I could smell his foul breath.

The monkey poked me hard in the chest and, hissing the song lyrics, he shoved me to the ground and pinned me down. While sitting on my chest, he and his chorus sang the rest of the song. Then he shot his vile sperm all over my face and laughed a hideous laugh that only something truly evil could produce. His head transformed into the round-spiked seedpod of the devil's weed, but there were no eyes or nose, just a huge mouth with sharp teeth and a drooling tongue.

"I am YOUR EXIT," the disgusting mouth said and bit me hard in the neck. But this was all my wolves could endure of my torture, and they jumped on the monkey and threw him off of me. Unfortunately, all of the other monkeys joined in, and a fierce battle began between my wolves and the army of monkeys. The head monkey had now recovered and was leering at me with death in his eyes.

Frantically looking around for a place to escape, I saw a ghostly image of a man who looked almost exactly like Don Vicente but was much older. He was standing on top of one of the burial mounds and was holding something dark in his right hand. He extended his hand toward me, and I ran as fast as I could toward him.

Time stopped all around me. I can tell you it was a freaky feeling having everything stop just like you pushed pause on a video—full-on *Matrix*-movie style—only me and the ghost-looking guy didn't stop like everything else. In fact, it seemed like he was the one who had paused the world.

When I reached him, he said not a word but bowed to me and then handed me an astonishingly beautiful knife made of pure obsidian. The black knife felt like pure magic, as though the stone was made for my hand. Sharper than a surgical scalpel, this was not only an incredibly fashioned piece of art, it was lethal by design and intention.

The world came back into motion, and the monkey "exit" came strolling toward me with the confidence of an experienced killer. Still licking my blood from his lips, he never saw the obsidian blade until it was too late for him. I stuck it deep in his chest and pulled it down all the way to his now-flaccid penis. Quickly and precisely, I disemboweled him just like I had done with deer in the past for food.

His last words were, "I am the exit. You have just walked through a door to another world, and you can never go back." The light show ended, the other monkeys disappeared, and Exit lay dead before me.

Holding the monkey's innards, I couldn't believe what I had done. "Don Vicente," I said with shaking hands and voice, "how could I have done this? I never wanted to kill a monkey. I had no intention in my heart to kill anything, especially something this beautiful and magical."

"First things first," he replied as he went and dug up my urn. "In order to fully remove a spell cast by a powerful brujo, you must make the brujo confess to what they have done. Many brujos have gone to their death after they had been caught but would not confess. This type of evil magic has always been considered a mortal sin by all cultures, and here in the Tuxtlas it is punishable by death. However, in this case I witched you in the sacred place of my ancestors so that you could learn, not to harm you. Therefore, I can confess for what I did without fear of retribution."

Don Vicente then went into a rather lengthy confession of specifically what he had done to me, and if I had not just spent the previous three days with "spirits," I would have thought he was utterly mad as he spoke directly to them in the middle of the thick jungle, where if someone was spying on us they would have seen nothing except two men sitting there.

After his confession, Don Vicente poured the contents of the urn into the hole it came from and filled in the hole with soil. Then he rinsed it with some water and, putting the urn aside, he began, "There is more than one reason that you took the monkey's life. First of all, the gallbladder of the monkey you are now holding is the antidote and protection for witching by los brujos negros. By killing the exit to obtain the gallbladder and my confessing, you are now free from the spell. After we leave here, you must let the bladder dry in the sun and make a fine dust of it that you will carry always in your takwatsi. This powder, obtained in the ritual way you have just performed, is the most powerful protection from evil spells of los brujos negros.

"This in itself is a great accomplishment for you and raises you to the next level of both curandero and brujo. But I also think that monkey chose to die by your hand for another reason."

"What could that possibly be?" I asked, still sobbing somewhat.

"Take your knife and open the bladder."

I did as Don Vicente said. As he peered inside, he let out a loud and almost cheerful "*Ha!* I was right."

Not knowing what in the world he was so happy about, Don Vicente proceeded to show me that the gallbladder was full of stones; more than likely, this monkey didn't have much more time to live. Instead of dying a miserable death, it had chosen to die a quick and honorable death as a warrior. "You did him a favor, and he gave you the precious gift that you came here for. The gall is the ultimate protection. This has turned out better than I could have ever hoped," he said with a grin and patted me gruffly on the back.

Don Vicente had me place the gallbladder in the urn to carry it back so I could dry it upon our return. Still holding the obsidian knife, I asked him about it.

"You must guard that knife with your life," Don Vicente replied. "When it is your time to leave this physical body and return it to the earth, the knife must be buried with you. It was given to you by the soul of my teacher, Don Genero." Don Vicente peered straight into my eyes and added, "One day you may give that knife away to someone in the same fashion Don Genero gave it to you. But until that day, the knife will be one of your most powerful and useful processions."

"I don't understand," I replied, perplexed by his cryptic words.

"You see, James, the arrival of the exit—in your case, the Lord of the Monkeys—would normally have been the beginning of the evil spell I cast on you. The exit would have ripped open your soul without actually killing you. That is what los brujos negros do. They injure a person's soul so that they suffer greatly and are never the same unless they find someone with the knowledge to cure them. But since you were in the graveyard of my ancestors, they helped you, as I was hoping they would. My benefactor gave you his precious knife so that your soul would not be damaged. But even with the knife, the only way of protecting yourself was to kill the spell, the exit, which you did. You rose to the occasion and proved yourself worthy of the gift Don Genero gave you. You have passed a great test, but more importantly you now have both the gall and the knife that kills the exit. You now have the protection and the cure for the most evil spell of los brujos negros, and I'm guessing they will come in very handy in the future."

With that said, we packed up our things and began the long walk home. Possibly the oddest thing among the whole phantasmagoric incident was Don Vicente humming the Nine Inch Nails song on the way back through the jungle.

———

los brujos de muerte

What I really wanted after my "trip" in the jungle was a long shower, some chiropractic work, a deep-tissue massage, and maybe a hot tub with a glass of wine after a nice meal. What I got instead was the fiercest continuation into brujería that I ever could have imagined. Before we even got back, we were stopped on the trail about half an hour from town by a dozen people who were clearly in panic mode and searching desperately for Don Vicente.

When they saw us and came running up, they all started talking at the same time, and much of what they were saying was in a Nahuatl dialect I didn't understand well. While looking over the small crowd, I saw an unexpected sight: Marisol. But it wasn't Marisol—it was like Marisol with all the life sucked out of her. Instead of the energetic and flamboyant woman I knew, what I saw was a woman with her head hung low and in obvious despair. She didn't even seem to realize I was there.

When I came up to her and gave her a hug, she was clearly surprised and fiercely hugged me back for a long time with her head buried in my chest. As she finally looked up into my eyes, I could somehow see into her soul; I saw that on a metaphysical level she was much more than I ever knew, and also that she was currently going through something tragic in the rational world.

On our way back to town, I learned from Marisol that a second cousin of hers, a teenage girl named Gabriela, had been brutally murdered in Veracruz City and that the prime suspect in the murder was none other than Rafael. But even though many people, including the police, knew it was him, they would do nothing for fear of the repercussions of his father, Don Julio, who was well known as a curandero/brujo in all of Mexico. The people knew that one way or the other, Rafael would pay for what he did.

The ironic thing about this situation was why Rafael had done it—it was simply to move up the ladder in brujería and attain more power. The taking of a person's life, in the ancient way of los brujos de muerte, was the ultimate means of gaining more life force, more power. And from what Marisol told me, Rafael did the deed in the specific way of the brujería: first he found a virgin and seduced her, then raped her, and then he cut out her still-beating heart, ate half of it, and stuffed the rest down her throat.

In other circumstances, like reading a book at home on my comfortable couch, this whole scene would just probably float across my mind like some horror movie or fiction book—but this was actually happening to me. I was still covered in now-dry monkey blood—and nobody even seemed to notice or care—and now I was talking to a friend who was telling me that her relative had been raped and killed and had her heart removed and eaten. The most disturbing part was that my consciousness had been altered so radically that I wasn't really fazed a bit.

Smacking myself in the head, trying to make sure I wasn't still dreaming, Don Vicente caught up to us on the trail and began his instructions. Pulling us aside, he first looked me in the eyes and said, "Don't get distracted by this beautiful young witch." His tone was fatherly, and he obviously used the term *witch* for his daughter in a kind and respectful manner. Then he turned his gaze to Marisol and said, "We have a lot of work to do. Pick up your spirit allies and take them with you as we make our journey to see what to do with Rafael. For you and James, this type of situation is where curanderos and brujos learn their lessons, and it is a very important part of your training to see what will happen."

Don Vicente abruptly walked away to join the crowd, but Marisol and I just stood on the trail watching them leave, unsure of what to do.

We eventually followed the group, and Marisol and I made it back to Don Vicente's house. On the way there, Marisol finally acknowledged that I was covered in monkey blood. When I asked her how she knew it was the blood of a monkey, she knowingly said that there is only one smell like it, and it wasn't just a monkey, it was the exit.

"Do you have it?" she asked.

"What?"

As fast as lightning, Marisol turned and grabbed my arm so tightly I thought she might break it.

"DO YOU HAVE IT?" she yelled in my face.

"Yeah, I have it."

"Good," she calmly replied, taking in a sigh of relief. "We're gonna need it."

I was going to let go of the whole scene that had just happened and simply walk on, but I couldn't.

"*Why* are we going to need it?"

Without stopping, missing a step, or even flinching, Marisol resolutely said, "We are going now to deal with the brujos de muerte—the witches of death—who are the deadliest beings of all three worlds. Rafael is now one of them. We are going to need the protection of what you carry in your urn that you haven't even shown me yet but that I know you now possess, and the gift from the dead that you must have received if you killed the exit. But using the powers of the exit and of the dead are dangerous and could mean our exit ..." I could tell she was now silently crying, but I didn't say anything in reply.

Don Vicente showed me how to dry the exit's gall, and while he was away for two days making preparations to catch Rafael, Marisol taught me many things, including how to make the gall into a fine powder. When the powder was finally complete, Marisol had us both pack our sacred items and say prayers to our allies for our dangerous mission. Then we left to meet Don Vicente in Veracruz City. Marisol said that it was extremely important that we fly to Veracruz City undetected, and she dressed both of us in very convincing disguises; in fact, her disguise was so complete that I barely recognized her. But when

I questioned her about the need for the disguises and why she said we were going to fly when I knew for sure that we were taking a bus to the city, she simply replied that it was not her place to explain it all to me and that Don Vicente would teach me more about those things when the time was right. "Flying with me to Veracruz City is my father's way of teaching you without words," Marisol said with her typical confidence now fully restored.

Dressed as important business people in impeccably tailored suits and carrying important-looking briefcases, Marisol and I took the first-class bus to the city. The word *fly* seemed to somehow fit perfectly, as being in my disguise and seeing Marisol's complete transformation had definitely altered my state of consciousness to the point where I almost didn't feel that I was even *me* anymore. It was as if I was flying through some sort of a dream or a movie scene. However, my curiosity over what was happening was overwhelming, and I couldn't help but try to get more answers from Marisol.

In retrospect, I should have just kept my mouth shut, for the answers that Marisol provided churned my stomach and caused a shaking fright throughout my entire being. One of the questions I asked her was what Don Vicente had been doing in the city for the last two days. I thought it was a fairly innocent question.

"My father has three main purposes now that the family of Gabriela has asked for his help. He must protect Gabriela's body, he must find Rafael, and he must gather the other curanderos and brujos to be witness to what to do with Rafael."

"But why does he need to protect her body?"

In a whisper, Marisol replied, "When a witch of death kills a person, for whatever reason, they ultimately desire to take the dead person's life force to make their own power greater. Killing the person is only the first step. Once the victim is dead, the corpse is allowed to rot, and after a few days the witch will come back to the body and suck the decaying juices of the corpse with a straw. This juice is what the witch of death desires more than anything. The witch also collects skin scrapings from the victim's fingertips, removing the fingerprints. Even in ancient times, witches knew that each person had unique fingerprints. By stealing them, the witch takes away the victim's unique markings and completes the theft of their soul. That is why Gabriela's body needs to be protected; the witch of death must not be allowed to complete his work and steal her soul. But Rafael is not the only one that my father may have to deal with. When a witch of death makes a kill, the other witches of death are somehow aware of it, and they will be drawn to the body in order to also suck the juices. This activity gives them power and also unites the group of witches like a pack of lions feeding on an antelope."

"So why did Rafael let her body be found?"

"I don't think he did. I don't know the whole story yet, but most likely something went wrong for Rafael. The witch of death will meticulously hide the corpse once he has killed. Rafael must have been seen by someone or got caught with her, or maybe she was a witch too and her teacher or someone else felt or dreamed what had happened to her; I don't know. But whatever happened, the family must have the body now if they asked my father to protect it. That's bad news for Rafael; it's the worst thing that could have happened to him. Without completing what he started, he will be drained of energy, and the other witches will be angry. Even though the witches of death are evil, they still have a code of conduct, and killing someone is not taken lightly. To kill someone and then not complete the rite is a mortal sin usually punished by death."

Just before pulling into the bus station, Marisol told me to secretly reach into my briefcase, locate my obsidian knife, and feel the power of the many ancestors who had wielded it in the past. As I did what she said and clearly felt that power running through me, I could also feel my confidence rising that I could deal with whatever this situation with Rafael would throw at me. Marisol also held something briefly in her hands before we arrived, but I didn't see what it was. All I know is that when we left the bus, I had never seen her more determined or full of energy. It was completely amazing that with thousands of people around us, no one knew how powerful of a witch Marisol was. To the masses, she appeared as simply one of them, but I knew differently.

———

Cornered in the end of a back alley in Veracruz City in the middle of the night, Rafael was surrounded by a group of powerful curanderos and brujos carrying torches and accompanied by their allies. For some reason, maybe because of the presence of so many curanderos and brujos or maybe due to an altered state I was experiencing, I could for the first time visually see all the allies of the others. Ravens, toads, cats, lizards, bats, wolves, bears, and cobras were all waiting at attention to see what was required. It was literally a zoo of spirit allies.

Outwardly, and to any non-witches that might have seen him, Rafael seemed completely confident and showed no fear. But those of us who could see his spirit allies knew that he and they were mortally afraid. They cowered behind him like frightened little children. By contrast, my allies were totally relaxed. Itzamna was actually joking around with the other spirit dwarfs while playing with my cougar's tail. They all seemed to be in party mode, but I was completely mortified by the whole scene.

Then came Don Vicente and Marisol. As they walked into the alley, all went silent and the playing was over. Staring at him straight in the eyes the whole time until she reached him, Marisol strode right up to Rafael. Her stare seemed to immobilize him, and she kicked him so hard in the groin that even I could feel it.

Rafael's allies finally rose up, but they were not even close to mounting a battle with those surrounding them. Pitifully and in accordance with Rafael's cowardly character, his allies did nothing to protect him.

With a single slight movement of his chin toward Rafael, Don Vicente sent in the whole group's allies, and within seconds Rafael's allies were dead, and he was all alone. My white wolf was licking her chops afterwards, but my cougar had a disappointed look on his face.

Kind of laughing to myself that Itzamna had distracted my cougar so he didn't get to feed, I turned to see a monkey high up in a light pole behind us. But just then Don Vicente addressed Rafael.

"You have poisoned, raped, and even killed, but your allies still had little power. That means you have no power. James, give him the exit and put this poor excuse of a brujo out of his misery and out of our sight!"

I couldn't believe what was now happening. There were clearly other curanderos and brujos there with a lifetime more experience than I had in this manner. Why did he pick me? I didn't even know what to do. Marisol backed off from Rafael, and as she walked by me she actually playfully slapped me on the ass as if I were a soccer or football player sent in to save the game. To my utter dismay, all of the other witches laughed like crazy. Itzamna was jumping up and down like a monkey.

In my hesitation, Marisol came back to me. "He poisoned you with the devil's weed, and then like a coward he raped and killed a poor girl—*my cousin*! Give him the exit or I will do it for you."

Groveling on the ground, Rafael didn't seem to pose any threat to me, plus his allies all lay dead around him. So I removed the small glass container holding the powdered gall of the exit from my takwatsi, and my allies and I walked up to Rafael.

"If you come any closer, I will kill you, gringo!" Rafael hissed with madness.

But my allies were not even phased one bit. In two seconds, my wolves had him on the ground with his arms pinned, and my giant cougar was sitting on Rafael's chest, licking his neck. My other allies stood watching, and I saw a glint in Ronnie's eye as he thought of picking Rafael's flesh.

As I took out the exit powder, suddenly Don Vicente yelled, "Make him confess first for what he has done. Or if he has done nothing wrong, then let him speak his truth and we may let him go."

All the allies cackled, and Itzamna continued to jump up and down, laughing like he was at a carnival watching the clowns.

Rafael replied in a terrified voice, "I did nothing wrong, and I have killed no one. I swear."

Suddenly all the allies and the curanderos and brujos stood silently still, as if Rafael had just signed his death warrant. The monkey I saw earlier sitting on the light pole came striding up to us and transformed into Don Julio, Rafael's father. "Give me the exit," he commanded me.

I brought forth the container of the exit's gall and he laughed at me. "That's not the exit, that's your gift for not being a coward like my son. That gall powder is your protection and the proof that you could endure the test of our ancient teachers. You spent three days in that burial ground with the devil's weed in your head, and you came out with the gall to prove it."

Kicking Rafael in the ribs, he continued, "This brujo pequeno lasted about an hour in that jungle cemetery and pissed his pants before he ran home screaming for his mommy. But that is *not* why he is being punished here tonight. He is being punished because he was given the chance to tell the truth in front of all of us, and he chose to lie. Many of us standing here have killed another person for one reason or another. It is a cruel world that way. But we do not lie about it.

"Maybe even if Rafael told the truth, we would still take his life for what he has done. Maybe if he stood his ground and spoke his truth, he would simply be punished. But now we will never know."

With a sigh but a resoluteness to his voice, he asked me again to give him the exit. This time I knew what he wanted, and from my takwatsi I pulled out the obsidian knife and handed it to him.

Marisol and Don Vicente came and led me away with all the others to leave Don Julio and his son.

It was never reported what happened to Rafael, and that's probably for the best. But he was never seen again, and everyone close to the situation knew why. Don Julio did the hardest thing a man could ever do, and that's why he's still one of the most respected curanderos in the world.

———

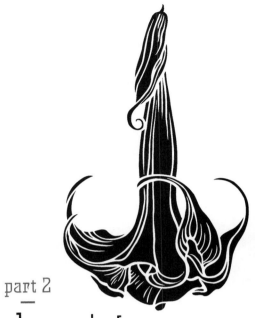

part 2
—
flying, dreaming,
and the devil's weed

florinda

ime to wake up, little brujo," I heard a singsongy female voice say as I felt someone gently shaking my shoulder. Slowly rubbing my eyes open, I found myself looking straight into the most mysterious set of eyes I had ever seen. They were like photos I'd seen of the earth taken from the moon—blue oceans and white clouds on a dark star-filled canvas. And just like a photo, these eyes did not blink, and I had the immediate sensation that I was staring into the eyes of some kind of magical cat that was intently focused on its prey.

I scrambled to a sitting position but had to keep myself from falling over as I suddenly realized I was in a hammock. With both hands gripping the sides of the hammock, I found myself face to face with a most extraordinary woman sitting on a cut log beside me. Even though she was sitting, I could tell she was probably very tall, maybe five feet ten or six feet in height. She had long, straight black hair and the high cheekbones and dark skin tone of the ancient races of Mexico. Old enough to easily be my mother, she nonetheless exuded a supremely youthful vitality, and when she smiled at me, her radiance and utter sensuality almost made me turn my head away.

"You've come a long way," I heard another voice say. I recognized Don Vicente's voice immediately. When I looked past the woman, I saw that he was standing in front of what appeared to be an open doorway, with the sunlight at his back making him appear as merely a silhouette against the light.

"Don Vicente," I said, happy to know that my teacher was there. "Where are we, and how did we get here?"

"The answers to both those questions and many more will be answered by your new teacher. This is Florinda, and she will be your guide for the next part of your training. Florinda is a master dreamer and works exclusively with our tribe in dealings with the underworld. I have given you to Florinda for however long it takes for you to become proficient in flying and conscious dreaming. Good luck, my son."

Before I could say anything, Don Vicente turned, stepped through the doorway, and disappeared. I jumped from the hammock and raced to the doorway after him, but just as I reached the light, a firm hand grabbed me and pulled me back. Boy am I glad she did! What I first thought was a doorway was in reality a large opening in the cave wall we were in that opened onto a sheer cliff face overlooking the ocean. Completely startled by almost running out of the opening and falling off the four- or five-story-high cliff, I turned to survey where I really was. What I saw took my breath away.

Florinda and I were in the most exquisite cave. It was not at all dark and dreary, as the word *cave* implies, but just the opposite: this cave was formed inside volcanic rock and had openings as large as three or four men and some small enough just to sit in that were all naturally positioned in various places on the ocean side, allowing copious amounts of light into the cave.

In the right back corner of the cave was the hammock I had woken up in that was tied to the cave walls at either end. And about fifteen feet to the left side was a low table that was somehow mounted to the wall, a chair, and next to the table were supplies like firewood, fruit, water gourds, and blankets, all neatly stacked and arranged. Looking back to the table, I then noticed some beautifully crafted ceramic pots, bowls, cups, and wooden spoons that were stored in holes above the table. The ceramic items seemed to be fashioned of the same type of rock as the cave and so were barely noticeable in their naturally made cupboards. All in all, while looking around the cave in astonishment, the one thought I had was that this place was the perfect cave that little boys and girls make in their rooms out of sheets and blankets or whatever they can find in order to have their own little private, make-believe world away from parents and school and responsibility. But this was no make-believe cave.

Florinda casually spread out a colorful blanket in the center of the cave floor and motioned for me to sit with her. In that moment, my being mesmerized by the cave gave way to a thousand questions of just what in the heck I was doing there.

"I realize you have lots of questions, but you must be patient. Not all of this can be learned or understood all at once,"

Florinda said in her captivating and melodious voice. "What we are going to do together will take time and immense concentration—concentration in ways that you have never experienced before."

"How do you know what I have experienced?" I asked, somewhat defensively.

"That's simple. If you had any clue what I was talking about, I wouldn't have to be here teaching you."

Well, she sure had me there, and I didn't argue.

"I'm going to give you an easy exercise to start with," Florinda said.

From a small bag she was carrying, she produced a paper figure about ten inches long that was folded and cut into the shape of a standing person that had strange hands, feet, and a head. Although it was very crude looking, I could tell right away that it was expertly crafted by someone who was a master at paper cutting.

"I made this for you so that you could focus your intention on copying it," Florinda said as she handed the paper figure to me. "There are sheets of paper over there on your desk for you to use. Any paper that you fold or cut while practicing, you should burn until you get it right. Then I will return."

With a light but loving stroke of my hair as she stood up, Florinda proceeded to walk up to and then through the same doorway that Don Vicente had, and then she vanished, just as he had.

I sat there holding the paper figure and for a moment felt a deep madness at myself for not finding out more about where I was, how I got there, why I was there, who Florinda was, and how in the world both Don Vicente and Florinda could walk out of the cave through a doorway in a cliff some fifty feet above the rocky coast below us.

But that feeling didn't last long, as throughout the years I was becoming accustomed to witnessing and experiencing feats of the unexplainable. So I let my feelings of frustration go and focused on the paper figure. The sooner I replicated it, the sooner Florinda would return and I could find out more.

However, the figure turned out to be much more difficult than I anticipated. I tried dozens of times to fold and cut the paper in the same way, but I simply couldn't figure it out. It seemed so simple, but it was deceptively intricate. Finally, discouraged and now hungry, I ate some of the fruit left for me and drank some of the water. In a few hours night would be closing in, so I got a small fire going and tried several more times to replicate the paper figure, but to no avail. When sunlight diminished and darkness came, I found it practically impossible to work with the paper. But now I had another problem: I needed to go to the bathroom. And, with that thought, I again became momentarily mad at myself for not thinking about that earlier or asking Florinda what to do. Looking out the doorways and windows of the cave, I saw no safe way out and now wondered even more just how I had gotten into the cave in the first place. The cliffs below and above the caves were sheer, and even though I was experienced in rock climbing, I was loath to try my skills on the cliff, especially in the dark and with no safety gear at all. But I also did not want to relieve myself in the cave.

Standing at the opening that my teachers had stepped through, and listening to the waves crash in the darkness, I had the overwhelming feeling of being trapped. I paced around the cave knowing that both Don Vicente and Florinda knew I would come to this situation, so there must be a solution. I could, of course, just pee off the side of the cliff, but that wouldn't help with what else I needed to do. In the past, while spending many days and nights on mountaineering treks climbing the cliffs of various mountains, I had used a bag that was specifically made for the purpose, but I had no such waste bag or container in the cave.

With my frustration level rising both from the inability to relieve myself and the feeling of not being able to even leave the cave, a wave of desperation began to take hold of me. I felt claustrophobic and jailed—two feelings that I utterly despise. And in my turmoil I decided that Don Vicente would not leave me in a situation that I had no chance of escaping, so I instinctively decided to try the only way I knew how to get out of the cave: to climb down the cliff. But just as I put one foot out of the doorway, I heard a familiar screech behind me. As I turned back toward the fire, my ally Ronnie, the eagle, stood staring at me and cocking his head back and forth.

"You don't need to climb," I heard Ronnie's voice say in my mind. "You can fly with me. The top of this cliff is not far up. Or we can go wherever else you like."

Thinking about what Ronnie said got me even more frustrated. "Ronnie," I replied, "when I fly with you, I fly with my consciousness, not my physical body. The need I have right now is to relieve my physical body. You can't possibly help with that."

"That's not entirely correct," I heard Florinda say as I looked over toward the cave openings and saw her standing there in the firelight.

"And that is one of the reasons you are here. Until now, you have always felt that you can only travel and fly in your dreams. I am here to teach you that this is not altogether true."

With an unexplainable amount of force and strength, Florinda walked over to me, picked me up, carried me to the doorway, and threw me out. As she threw me, she yelled, "All you have to do is fly to your bathroom."

And that's exactly what happened. I was standing in front of the mirror in the master bathroom of my house in Arizona. The first thing that came to my mind was that, of course, I was dreaming all of this. But that certainty starting slipping away as I closely examined the bathroom and leafed through the magazines in the rack. It all seemed so utterly real. After I was finished with my business, I even washed my hands before I found myself back in the cave lying down—with Florinda pouring water on my head.

"What the heck are you doing?" I yelled at her.

Stepping back from me as I lay on the ground, she replied, "I had to bring you back. You would have stayed there if I let you; you are not ready for that yet. We must take this in small steps. You did wonderfully—better than I even expected—but you still lack discipline. Go to sleep now and continue working with your figure tomorrow. I'll be back soon."

"Soon" to Florinda was definitely different than "soon" for me. I spent the next two days and nights in the cave trying to replicate the paper figure, but for some reason I couldn't get it exactly right. When I became frustrated or bored, I would stand for hours looking out the doorways and windows of the cave and out into the ocean. Ronnie came and visited me a few times to see if I needed to "fly" and relieve myself, but my diet of fruit was more like fasting to me, and I had no need.

Still, on the third day, I got so frustrated with the paper figure that I tossed it and all the other paper in the cave into the fire and announced, with some vulgarity, that I was finished.

———

flowers of magic

o my utter surprise, I awoke in a comfortably soft bed in an exquisitely furnished room of what looked to be antique furniture. I felt like I was in the bedroom of a wealthy landowner in a great hacienda of the sixteenth or seventeenth century. The bedroom was as enormous as the bed, and as I arose I saw clean clothes and a washbasin laid out on a bureau next to the bed.

But I didn't make it there. As soon as I got up, I fell down. The pain in my head was so excruciating that I went blind and my legs buckled beneath me. Suddenly I felt strong arms lifting me, and I was seated back on the bed. When I could finally see again, Florinda was sitting next to me, handing me a glass of pinkish water that I immediately drank right down. She gently rubbed my shoulders, arms, and then temples, and within minutes my headache had miraculously subsided, and I felt rested and relaxed. I asked Florinda how in the world I could go so quickly from feeling incredibly awful to feeling perfectly fine.

"I gave you the antidotes for the stramonium," Florinda replied. "The pink drink is made from the salvia cactus and rose water, and the healing touch of a dreamer never hurts either," she said in a playfully mocking voice.

"What is stramonium?" I asked.

"It's a type of datura, silly," she replied and, continuing her playful mood, she gently socked me in the shoulder.

Florinda's jovial mood was intoxicating, and I feigned falling over from her massive punch. Laughing while sitting back up, I told her that I was not familiar with the term *stramonium,* and she sarcastically rolled her eyes and shook her head.

"For someone with so much experience flying, you really lack knowledge of the sacred plants. Well, I guess that's another reason Vicente sent you to me. Okay, here's the plan: you wash up and change clothes, and I'll meet you in the kitchen in a few minutes. We'll have a bite to eat and then I'll take you to the gardens, where we can talk."

After quickly washing and changing, I found myself walking down a long hallway with many doors on each side. As I had guessed, the house was massive, but I found the central kitchen without a problem. Florinda and I ate some delicious tamales, and then I followed her out a set of French doors and into the most amazing garden of flowers I had ever seen.

Most of the huge flowers were shaped very similar to each other, and I recognized one of the species right away as the datura that grew wild in the area where I lived in Arizona. With that realization, it suddenly became apparent to me that all the various species of flowering plants in the garden were probably related and that they were all some sort of sacred datura. I was completely blown away by what I was seeing, and Florinda most have known that because she simply let me wander through the garden and take it all in on my own.

The beautiful white-flowered daturas that I knew were simply one of dozens of similar plants of various sizes, shapes, and colors. Some were yellow and double cupped, some were white with purple in the middle, and some were brilliant purple with white in the middle. All of them were funnel shaped, a distinct characteristic of the datura. Continuing to walk around the back of the garden, my heart almost stopped as I looked up at another set of species that were similar but also radically different. The daturas in the front of the garden were bushes from about three to six feet high and flowers about three to five inches in length, but the plants in the back were enormous and resembled trees that grew over ten feet tall, with the largest flowers I had ever seen—some over a foot long with yellow, red, white, cream, and multicolored flowers that were so spectacular, they hardly seemed real. The funnel-shaped flowers were so large on these plants that they actually bent forward to the point of hanging upside down.

As I stood mesmerized in front of a plant with the largest and most abundant flowers (dark orange to light orange and white, almost two feet long) that was the tallest in the garden at almost twenty feet high, Florinda came and stood next to me. After a few moments, she introduced me to the plant.

"James, this is Be Very. Be Very, this is James," Florinda said happily. "Be Very is my little pet name for her that is short for the name of her species: *Brugmansia versicolor*. I found her relatives in Ecuador and brought the seeds back to grow and live with us here. Although, as you guessed correctly, many of the species in this garden are datura, these larger species are now normally classified as brugmansia because of their tree-like growth. Most people grow them for their beautiful flowers and call them angel's trumpets, but don't let the name fool you. Just as the *Datura inoxia*, with the unique funnel-shaped white flowers that you know well, all the species of angel's trumpet, or brugmansia, are also sacred plants with the power to alter human perception and must be treated with respect if you ingest them, or you can go crazy or even die."

Upon hearing her reminder about the potency of all the beautiful flowering plants surrounding me, a chill went down my spine, and for some reason I almost felt like running away. But again Florinda somehow sensed my mood or thoughts and gently took my hand and walked me back toward the front of the garden and to a much shorter plant with the smallest flowers in the garden.

"This is *Datura stramonium*," Florinda announced. "Stramonium here will be your guide for the first part of our time together."

Beautiful, but certainly not the most impressive-looking plant in the garden, stramonium had a very peculiar feeling and smell to it. The best way to describe it is that it seemed on one level to be very harsh, as it had toothed leaves that were different from the smooth-edged leaves of the other daturas, but on another level, the five-peaked funnel-shaped flowers seemed almost whimsical, and the whole plant appeared to be radiating a violet aura.

"I'm surprised you don't know more about the history of this plant," Florinda said as she looked down on me with a quizzical face and I became fully aware of how much taller she was than me.

"People call the stramonium the jimsonweed, which came from the name Jamestown weed. Even though it now grows all around the globe, it originated in what is now the northeast part of the United States, near where you were born. As you probably know, Jamestown was one of the first British colonies in North America, founded in the early 1600s. What you don't know is that by the late 1600s the aristocratic colonists and their servants had formed an uprising against the British. When the British soldiers came to Jamestown, they had little food, and since they were enemies of the Indians, an Algonquian Indian witch cast a spell on them to eat the stramonium as a salad. And so for many days the soldiers were out of their minds, haplessly wandering around, playing jokes on each other, and urinating and defecating on themselves. Luckily for the soldiers the Algonquian witch did not intend to kill them, and so no one died or even acted maliciously, but that is how stramonium became known as Jamestown weed. The sad thing is that not long after that incident, the soldiers burnt the whole town of Jamestown to the ground."

Contemplating her story, Florinda interrupted my thoughts by saying rather dramatically, "Okay, now for some real lessons. James, obviously the shape of the flowers are similar, but what is the most striking difference between the brugmansia and the datura besides their size?"

Florinda must not have noticed that I had been so enthralled by the various species, her question was simple for me to answer. "The seedpods of the brugmansia have no prickly spines, but all of the seedpods of the various datura do."

"Very good observation, and that is why the brugmansia is so tricky. The prickly datura pods are screaming 'danger, don't eat me,' but the brugmansia gives no such warning. For that and other reasons that you will learn in time, we will continue your training with the datura, which is very straightforward. Specifically, you will first learn the ways of the stramonium. Come now, and pick five seedpods from the stramonium while telling the plant that you honor it and mean no harm."

Doing as Florinda instructed, I picked the seedpods and then followed her back to the kitchen, where she exited out a side door I hadn't noticed before. We ended up in a small courtyard encircled by a high stone wall. In the middle of the courtyard was a large, round fire pit about four feet in diameter dug into the ground with a copper-looking piece of metal run around the outside. A nice crackling fire was already burning, and I silently wondered who had built it since I had not seen nor heard any other people in the house.

———

flying with the witches

lorinda motioned for me to sit by the fire, and then she went into a flurry of activity that she performed so gracefully it was as if I was witnessing a kind of sacred dance. Seemingly without any effort, she pulled over and put on the fire a large iron grate that was shaped in a circle and had four legs about two feet high. On top of that she placed a round iron pot, and after disappearing around the corner for a few moments, she filled the pot with a liquid that smelled like a fragrant form of *tesguino* (a brewed corn beverage). And, lastly, she produced a magnificent mortar and pestle set that she placed in front of me.

Florinda sat down next to me and, handing me a sharp knife, instructed me to carefully cut open one of the seedpods, which were oblong and about two inches long and a little less wide. There were four chambers inside the pod, and I immediately thought how cool it was that the seedpod mirrored the four directions; when I looked over to Florinda, she simply raised her eyebrows knowingly and said nothing. However, it was from that moment on that I knew Florinda and I shared a special connection. I don't know if she was simply very perceptive or actually psychic; the fact remained that she seemed to know my thoughts, and in some cases I also knew hers.

I cut open four more seedpods, making a total of five, and scraped the seeds into the mortar. As I crushed them with the pestle, Florinda began speaking. "You are a skilled dreamer with powerful allies from the underworld, James. And Vicente has told me about your experiences with the witches here in the Tuxtlas. I have no doubt that your previous teachers throughout the years have been knowledgeable and credible; in fact, you may be surprised to know that I am well acquainted with one of them from far away, and now we have a little surprise for you."

Immediately a wave of excitement filled me, and somehow I just knew what was going to happen next. In a millisecond, I remembered the delicious tamales that were prepared for us and the fire that was already lit. The manner in which both were prepared was very familiar to me, but I hadn't consciously known why. But now I absolutely did.

Xilonen, my old friend and teacher from Oaxaca (some 300 miles away), came out through the French doors with her colorful Mazatec dress flowing and her always-vibrant eyes glowing. I stood up to greet her and a flood of emotion overtook me as she hugged me tight to her large bosom.

Upon sitting down with us, Xilonen said, "I was not surprised to learn you were here with my compadres, the witches of Los Tuxtlas. It is a path I did not see for you but one that is a natural progression. It is good to have various teachers and mentors. Many years ago I was Florinda's dreaming teacher, and now she is yours. You must remember when I was teaching you curing through dreaming I used the paper figures, but I told you I could not teach you how to make them. That was because it was not my place to do so. Now that you have made it here, you will learn the figures with Florinda, for that is the rule: one generation must teach the next. My teacher taught me, I taught Florinda, and Florinda will teach you. The rule is set that way because each master of a new generation adds his or her own touch and that keeps the traditions alive and current. Florinda is a master dreamer and healer of her generation, and it is her task to train the new generation. In a way, she is now your mother, and I am your grandmother."

In her comical manner, Florinda added, "And that makes Vicente your father, Marisol your sister, and Julio your uncle. In fact, you now have lots of new relatives: grandparents, aunts and uncles, sisters and brothers, cousins and nieces and nephews. We are all one big happy family!"

The old witches laughed heartily, and I was not only amazed but thoroughly intrigued at how lightly they both handled what for me was a very serious situation. It was almost frightening that Xilonen, my Mazatek teacher from Oaxaca, was here in Veracruz in the very house of my new teacher, Florinda. It was so surreal, my mind was barely keeping up. So I guess I shouldn't have been surprised at what happened next: Marisol had somehow snuck up behind me and poked me in the ribs!

Now I had *three* generations of witches laughing at me.

Well, actually, they were laughing *with* me—it didn't take long for me to join in their mirth, and soon we were all holding our sides and trying to stop laughing. It took awhile, but finally the laughter subsided, and Marisol, still giggling and wiping tears from her eyes, said to me, "Well, maybe these two grumpy old witches are finally ready to teach us something."

"Watch your manners, young lady," Xilonen said jokingly. "Or would you like me to turn you into a toad?" The ironic and sarcastic tone to Xilonen's statement had us all rolling again, and I realized through my laughter that the absurdity of the situation was actually providing a feeling of kinship between all of us that was indescribable. I truly felt that we were family and, apart from everything else, there was a sincere love and respect between us all.

Marisol produced a bottle of rum from her jacket, took a swig, and spat it into the fire, causing a great flash, and everyone became silent, even though a sense of humor still filled the air. After a few minutes, Florinda told me to scrape the crushed stramonium seeds into the boiling liquid in the pot. I had the distinct feeling the three witches were secretly suppressing their laughter and were acting in a serious manner simply for my benefit. And, a few moments later, I had my suspicions verified when Xilonen turned to Marisol and harshly asked, "Well, what are you waiting for, you silly witch? Aren't you going to use our magical device to stir the potion?"

"Oh my gosh! I'm so sorry! I completely forgot!" Marisol said as she hastily got up and ran to a dark corner of the courtyard. When she returned carrying a miniature homemade straw broomstick and began stirring the pot with the wooden end, the three witches again roared with laughter. I joined them until we were finally all laughed out and lying on the ground.

"Do you know why witches are often portrayed as flying with broomsticks?" Florinda asked me as she sat up and tried to hold back more laughter. "It's because our ancestors were very practical and often used one tool for many things. For example, they used their brooms for sweeping, but they also used them for stirring, and quite naturally they used them for flying."

To my utter shock, Florinda grabbed the broomstick from the pot, blew on the end to cool it, and then sat back down with her legs spread open. She then lifted up her skirt and very slowly and carefully placed the sticky-wet end of the broomstick inside of her. I wanted to look away but couldn't.

"Don't be alarmed, James," Florinda said casually. "There is no reason to feel shy or ashamed. I am completely comfortable with my body, and I want you to see that. I have nothing to hide from you."

I was so astonished that I actually felt embarrassed.

Of course Florinda knew what I was feeling, and she chuckled as she told me, "Your thoughts right now are part of why you are here with us, James. You have been raised in a culture devoid of the mysterious aspects of life and death—where people hide their bodies under layers of clothes and go naked only under the covers. But even more importantly, they have forgotten the true power of our sexual organs. The clitoris and the head of the penis are our physical membranes that link us to the Divine. That is why we use them to fly. In the case of the datura brew, it is much safer to apply it to our membranes than to ingest it into our stomach. Watch me!"

Florinda proceeded to dip the broom handle many times into the pot and rub the liquid onto her most private of places. As she did, I slipped into an altered state of consciousness that I had never experienced before. The sheer impact and implications of the scene I was witnessing was overwhelming on so many levels, I thought for a moment that I might even pass out.

When Florinda was finished, she held the end of the broomstick over the heat of the fire for a minute to cleanse it and then passed it to Xilonen, who dipped it into the pot and proceeded to rub herself with the liquid, and then Marisol did the same. Even though I had been physically, intellectually, and emotionally attracted to Marisol since the moment we met, I was in such an altered state that watching her rub the liquid on herself produced absolutely no sexual feelings at all. The whole situation was so utterly bizarre that my normal thoughts and desires disappeared into the mysterious and unknown realms of these remarkable witches.

Handing the broom to me, I caught Marisol's eyes and something felt like it snapped at the base of my neck, and my normal awareness seemed to return. I jerked my head toward Florinda and Xilonen, searching for an answer. Thankfully, Xilonen replied, "You are one of us now, James. We three do not need the datura to fly, but we do it for you to welcome you to our tribe, and also because it is necessary for you to break open your mind. The three of us have all been born and raised with the knowledge of curanderos and brujos, but you were not. So for you, it is more of a struggle for your rational mind to let go to the mysteries and the unknown. That is why you need the datura as a guide. One day you will no longer need the datura or anything else in order to fly, but right now the spirit of the stramonium will help you to fly and consciously dream. Dip the broom into the pot and rub the liquid on yourself, and then let it dry. When it dries, rub some more on, and let it dry. Do that a total of five times."

When I had finished anointing my sexual organ, Florinda silently gestured to me to put the broom in the fire, and the four of us joined hands as we watched it burn. Knowing my thoughts, once again I heard Florinda's voice in my mind telling me not to be preoccupied with the significance or symbolism of the broom. She told me we were about to go on a magnificent journey, and as the four of us stared into the fire, I felt a rapid sleepiness engulf me. The next thing I remember is waking up in the ocean.

It was dark all around me, and I was tired and had a hard time keeping my head above the salty water that filled my mouth and nose. Doggy-paddling, I called out, but no one answered. On the horizon, I saw a small speck of light, so I tried swimming toward it. But after a while I simply couldn't swim anymore, and the blackness overtook me. When I awoke, I was washed up on the beach, and upon standing, I heard voices yelling far above me. It was my witch family, but I couldn't reach them. The cliff face was too sheer to climb in the dark.

In a blink, Marisol was beside me and holding my hand. Looking me in the eyes and brushing the hair back off of my face, she cheerfully explained to me that I was with the stramonium now—that I could fly if I wanted to. "Come on, you silly boy," Marisol said to me in a voice of a girl half her age. And with that, I was in the cave where I had first met Florinda, overlooking the ocean with Marisol, Xilonen, and Florinda.

———

meeting the spirits

Y ou have quite the flair for the dramatic, Ulu Temay," Florinda said, and everyone laughed as I sat down next to the fire with them.

"Why are you calling me by my Wirrarika name?" I asked.

"Because it's finally time for you to properly earn it!" I heard a deep male voice say as a strong gust of wind simultaneously came through the main doorway of the cave and blew the fire violently.

"Matziwa!" I exclaimed, as I could recognize the voice of my Wirrarika teacher from the Western Sierras anywhere. I had spent almost twenty years learning from the Wirrarika shamans, and Matziwa was one of my main and dearest teachers. He had taken me long ago as part of his family.

"Matziwa has passed you to us now," Xilonen said. "But the name you were given by this holy man and master of consciousness is one you are expected to live up to. Do you think you were given the name of 'New Arrow of the Sun' by whim or accident? Hardly! Arrows fly through the air with purpose, and that is what you will eventually learn to do."

"But first," Florinda added, "to fly with purpose, you must learn how to better control your dreaming. Years ago, Xilonen and the Wirrarika shaman Alberto taught you about dreaming, and Matziwa about flying; now the witches of the Tuxtlas are going to teach you even more. We are going to teach you about the airs."

I had heard about the concept of "airs" before; that spirits are referred to as "airs" or "winds" is common in Mesoamerican indigenous cultures. What I really wanted to know in that moment was if I was currently dreaming or awake, so I asked Florinda.

"Dreaming, yes," she replied with a cold stare. "But this is *so* much more than common, random dreams. With the help of us experienced witches, you are consciously dreaming a collective dream with us. This state of consciousness resembles much more closely your awake consciousness state than the random dreams of common sleep. You could call this state dreaming-awake if you like. Your task is to focus your attention while consciously dreaming, and by that means bring your conscious dreaming to the conscious awake world."

"You have already done this many times, Ulu Temay," Xilonen added. "When Matziwa and your many other teachers taught you how to connect with your spirit guides and when I taught you to fly in your condor body, you were consciously dreaming. Now we are going to show you how to go deeper. That is why Florinda asked you to work on re-creating the paper figure in this sacred cave. Creating the intricate paper figure while you are consciously dreaming serves two purposes. First, it focuses your attention to a super-high degree, and second, it allows you to bring a manifestation of the underworld, the dream world, back with you into your awake consciousness."

"Watch!" Marisol whispered vehemently to me while not-so-gently elbowing me in the ribs.

"Hey, Matziwa, you old mountain goat, I know you're still here, watching us. Show yourself to Ulu Temay," Florinda said out loud in her playful voice.

I was staring at the fire and waiting for something to happen when Marisol elbowed me again and shook her head at me like I was a little kid not paying attention. Looking up at her, she thrust her chin toward the cave wall. Astonishingly, there was an intricate shadow being cast on the wall, as if something was between the firelight and the cave wall—but I couldn't see anything that would make the shadow.

With lightning speed, Florinda took a small piece of paper from a stack next to her, and on a board about a foot square she folded and cut with an obsidian razor an exact replica of the shadowy figure on the wall.

Holding up the effigy, she yelled happily, "Ha! You old devil. I got you now!"

The shadow on the wall disappeared, and the paper figure in Florinda's hand suddenly became alive. Matziwa was somehow trapped in the figure, but he remained completely calm and said, "Okay, Florinda, you've had your fun now. Don't you think it's time to quit playing and get to work?"

"Fine, you grumpy old man," Florinda said lovingly, as if to her father, and threw the paper figure into the fire. With a laugh, Matziwa's shadow briefly appeared on the wall again and then flew out on a breeze from the sea.

"And that's how this works," Florinda said with a smile. "It's simple, really. Everything has a spirit and a soul. In dreaming you can learn to see the spirits. As you know, Matziwa is a master shaman and dreamer, so it's easy for us to see him if he wants to be seen. And you also well know from your time as his pupil that he can even be seen as himself just as if he were really here, even when his physical body is far away. All of us that have mastered the art can be seen in our spirit form if we choose. Do you think Xilonen traveled all the way here on a bus? The other spirits, especially those that don't have a human form, can also be seen and even controlled for our healing practices if you have enough intention or willpower. These are the spirits that help us curanderos with healing the injured souls of the people who come to us when they are sick."

"The best thing," Xilonen added, "is that once you know the form of a spirit, you can call it by simply making its figure. For example, Florinda could make another figure of Matziwa and he would be here right away. We are not going to bother him again tonight, but we surely could if we wanted to."

"We surely could!" Marisol added in her cheerfully adolescent voice.

This time Florinda playfully poked me in the ribs and whispered to watch Xilonen. Both Florinda and Marisol giggled like little girls at me and, in that moment, it finally dawned on me why they were poking me. I came up with two valid reasons.

First, it would be very easy to fall into some macabre mood at all the shadowy witchy stuff I was learning. And secondly, by continually "poking" me, they ensured that I stayed in the conscious dream state, or what they referred to as dreaming awake.

Playing along with this most serious of games, I quickly stood up, turned around, and mooned them all with my milky white buttocks.

The three witches cheered and applauded with delight as I sat back down. Of all the exceptional moments of my life, that moment is one that is singularly etched into my mind.

"Okay, crazy people," Xilonen said mockingly when we finally all stopped laughing and were staring at the fire. "Let's start Ulu Temay off with an easy one. The spirit of this cave is very nurturing and protective to human beings, and it is already here. Can you feel it?"

She rapidly folded and cut an image in paper while I whispered to Marisol a question about the paper, and she hurriedly told me that it was special paper called *amatl* that the witches made from the fig trees at the witches' house. I tried asking her more but she grabbed my left nipple so hard I almost squealed.

Focusing back on Xilonen, I saw that she had created a very simple figure of a person with the arms raised above the head and two triangles cut into the torso, one larger than the other. Looking at the figure, I intuitively knew that the large triangle represented the ocean below us and the smaller one the cave we were in.

Marisol handed me a board, a piece of amatl, and an obsidian razor. Amazingly, I folded and cut it almost exactly like Xilonen's on the first try. Florinda rapidly cut the figure also and called the name while holding it up to the fire. A light wind blew through the cave and a shadow of similar shape and form to Florinda's cut figure danced on the cave wall.

"Florinda has spent many years learning and working in this cave," Xilonen said. "She knows it like it is a part of her, and someday both you and Marisol will as well."

"Now," Florinda instructed, "feel the qualities of the figure and the shadow it casts, and tell me what it feels like."

For me, both the shadow and the figure felt very kind, nurturing, and even protective. Marisol had the same feeling and added that compared with the figure of Matziwa, the cliff-cave seemed very simple and uncomplicated, even innocent. While Marisol described what she felt, it was as if she were reading my mind, because I completely shared with her all the feelings that she was describing. Florinda was smiling and appeared to be very pleased. Remarkably, both Marisol's and my figures were very similar but in some way uniquely different from each other's and from Florinda's.

Florinda noticed this and explained. "The wind spirit of this cliff cave is a protector spirit, and for each of us that means something slightly different. As you will see, all of our figures for individual spirits will be very similar but also unique to the witch that is cutting them to bring them forth. The figure you have just cut can be used to invoke protection for you and your clients when doing healing work or whenever protection is needed."

"Why do you call the spirit a wind spirit?" I asked.

"The terms *wind* or *airs* can be used for all spirits, as that is what they are—or, more precisely, how they manifest here in these worldly dimensions," Florinda replied. "You see, James, whether a spirit is helping or hurting, good or evil, friendly or malevolent, each has its own air or quality or even smell that cannot be seen ordinarily. Just like the wind, we can see its effects and feel its distinct qualities, such as a hot desert wind or a salty ocean breeze. We can even smell where the air has been. But we don't actually see the air, do we? It's not visible. And that's why our ancestors devised this system of figures that give shape to the spirit airs, or winds. The figures focus our intention and give form to what we feel about the spirit wind. If we need or want to, we can see them with shadows from the light or in the smoke from a fire.

"Let's try another." Florinda cut another figure, much more intricate and beautiful, and held it up for us to see. "What is it?" she asked.

Marisol and I looked at each other and simultaneously said the word *star*, even though Florinda's figure was still in the typical human shape with legs, torso, arms, and head and did not in the least resemble the typical five-pointed shape that is usually drawn to represent a star in modern society. Although unique in many ways, the only real difference in the appearance of the star spirit figure was the intricately cut designs on the torso and heart areas. But just with these seemingly small variations, the figure basically screamed *star spirit* when looked upon.

"Like the fire or candle, the star, or *sitalij*, spirit is a light in the darkness, a guardian to witches, and a beacon for those who are lost. It is one of my favorite spirits to invoke when I am searching for the missing soul of a client. Now it's your turn to invoke it."

Marisol cut her star figure fairly quickly, but I took much longer as I tried my best to replicate Florinda's.

"James," Florinda said as she noticed my difficulty. "Simply look intently at my figure and capture it in your mind. Then cut what you feel the star being to be. It doesn't matter if it's exactly like mine or not; it's the feeling and presence that it invokes in you that is important."

What Florinda said helped tremendously, and I completed the star spirit figure in a few minutes. Again, it was astonishing how similar yet unique the three of our figures were. The three of us proceeded to cut and experience many more figures while Xilonen watching intently and added a comment or bit of wisdom now and again. We cut figures of flower spirits, love spirits, corn and other food spirits, and non-predatory animals, as well as many more guardian spirits. With each spirit figure we cut, Marisol and I would tell Florinda and Xilonen how the spirit felt to us, and then Florinda would give an in-depth explanation of her personal relationship to the spirit and how it was invoked in the healing arts. The concentration necessary to do all that was enormous, and after about twenty figures, I was beginning to lose focus, even though I was completely fascinated and did not want to stop.

"You have cut the prerequisite amount of figures from feeling the unique qualities of each spirit," Xilonen said, abruptly addressing Marisol and I. "Your teacher has done an impeccable job of summoning the spirits here for you, and now your real work begins by meeting the spirits in person and where they live. Have a nice flight!"

Xilonen clapped her hands, and the fire flashed. Blinking my eyes rapidly to regain my vision, I noticed Xilonen was gone. I closed my eyes fully and thought to myself that if I just kept them closed for a few moments until they readjusted from the flash, I would see Xilonen sitting there again, but when I opened them, I was no longer in the cave.

———

acquiring spirits

I woke up to the strong smell of coffee and, without really thinking about what I was doing or where I was, I walked out of my room and down the long hallway to the kitchen, where Marisol was cooking on the stove. I pulled up a chair at the counter in front of the cooking area, and Marisol nonchalantly poured me a cup of coffee and went back to what she was cooking, which smelled fantastic. With the first sips of strong coffee, I realized how famished I was.

Suddenly a flood of memories of the cave hit me. The memories seemed so real I had a hard time believing I had been dreaming. I asked Marisol how long I had been asleep.

"I wouldn't exactly say you were asleep," she replied and set a magnificent plate of food in front of me and then brought her own plate and sat next to me.

"What do you mean I wasn't exactly sleeping?" I asked her in between bites.

"You were conscious dreaming, dreaming awake, flying on the wings of perception, in a state of altered awareness—whatever term makes the most sense to you," she replied rather flippantly.

Just then, Florinda walked in from the garden and handed us both a glass of the pinkish salvia-rose drink. "This will help clear your heads and not be at each other's throats," she said to us like we were little children. "The concentration needed to invoke and experience as many different spirits as you both have in such a short period of time can tax even a seasoned witch and make them irritable to silly questions.

"Flying on the wings of perception, as Marisol has so eloquently put it, is one of the most complex states of mind that human beings can experience. But whether it is brought on by a plant ally such as the datura or by any other means, it takes its toll on you until you are accustomed to it."

"Why is that?" I asked Florinda. I began to feel much better with some food and her pink drink working its magic in me.

"Because that state of mind is the opposite of everything you've ever been taught."

Seeing that I still truly didn't get it, Florinda patiently explained, "The witchcraft you are learning is all about expanding your level of awareness to a much grander version of consciousness than you have ever before even imagined. The witches of our tribe do not limit themselves to the consensus of 'ordinary' reality. The consensus of what other people think is of little importance to us."

I looked over at Marisol and she nodded her head in agreement with Florinda. "But isn't this ordinary reality?" I asked.

"I'm sitting here with the two of you, eating chilaquiles and drinking coffee. That seems pretty ordinary to me."

"Of course," Florinda replied. "We are human beings and need to eat and drink, love and learn, walk and talk. What I am trying to show you is that there is infinitely more. We witches fly free because we have mastered the common affairs of life. That's not to say we never have problems or don't need to work hard at what we do. But, at the same time, we handle our every-day affairs in a manner that doesn't consume all of our energy, so that we have the ability and the time for more esoteric pursuits—for pursuits in other realms of consciousness that most of humanity has all but forgotten."

"But we don't feel better or above our fellow human beings," Marisol added. "We help them with our work of healing, and when the spirits put someone in our path that is ready to learn, then we teach them like we are teaching you."

The sincerity of Marisol and Florinda's words, coupled with all I had done and seen with them, brought me to tears in a flood of emotion. I drew them both to me with my arms and hugged them both.

A few moments later, after Florinda had indulged my emotional outburst, she laughed her familiar lighthearted laugh and told us we needed to start right away at meeting for ourselves the spirits we had invoked while being introduced to them during our three days in the cave. "Plus," she added, "the physical exercise will do you good."

"Three days!" I exclaimed. "I thought we were there only one night."

Marisol merely shook her head at me and chuckled.

"But I don't remember being there for three days," I complained. "I only remember it being dark in the cave, except for the fire. I have no memory of daytime."

"Don't worry," Florinda said gently. "It's common to experience conscious dreaming as a world of shadows when you are just beginning. And remember that you have never gone this deep into your dream state and that you were also affected by Xilonen and myself. Especially when around a flying witch like Xilonen, the awareness, perception, consciousness, and even the passage of time can be radically altered. Xilonen is gone now, but she has left you both a gift at the bench by the creek, where you will begin your lessons with the spirits. Go now and come back when you have spoken to the spirit of the creek."

———

Walking down the trail to the creek, I couldn't believe that three days had gone by while we were in the cave. "How is that possible?" I asked Marisol. "And did *you* know we were there for three days?"

"I can't explain it to you any better than Florinda just did. But, yeah, I knew how long we had been there before Florinda told us."

"So, how? Did you see the sun rise and set?"

"No, silly. Arturo came this morning with the milk delivery. He only ever comes on Thursday, and we went to the cave on Monday. Not everything is as complicated as you like to make it," Marisol said, appearing to be quite pleased with herself.

"Damn witches," I said while chuckling as we reached the bench by the creek.

Sitting on the bench were two beautifully handcrafted wooden boxes just long and wide enough to hold each of our paper spirit figures. Upon opening my box and seeing the figure of the creek spirit on top of the other cut figures, a flood of memories came all at once, and I had to sit down. "I don't remember bringing the figures we had cut out of the cave," I said with some exasperation.

"That's because we didn't," Marisol replied in a faraway voice, as if she was remembering something important. "Xilonen brought them for us because we still don't have the knowledge or power to bring physical objects to or from our dreaming consciousness."

Suddenly I too began remembering details of our time in the cave, especially of Florinda invoking the individual spirits for us and then of Marisol and me feeling them and cutting their figures. For example, I had no recollection until that moment of meeting the creek spirit with Florinda in the cave. But now that I saw the figure I had cut of it, I remembered every detail about how it made me feel. I was astounded that now that I was actually sitting by the creek, the feeling was identical.

Marisol seemed to be having similar memories and said, "Flying with the datura spirit is quite different than normal states of consciousness. I probably don't know a whole lot more about it than you do, but I've been around it my whole life, and what I do know is that when most people take it, they remember nothing afterwards—even if it's many days after. That's mainly because they didn't invoke the spirit with a clear purpose or have someone experienced guiding them. Mostly people foolishly try datura just to see what it feels like or because they've heard it is dangerous and want to experiment with it as some kind of a kick or a thrill. But when witches use it, they invoke the spirit in special ways that have been handed down through countless generations, and they always invoke it in a sacred place and in the company of other experienced witches. This is what is called proper use of set and setting: why you are doing it, with whom, and where. In our case, we were set up for a successful flight by our experienced teachers. They knew the strength of what we were taking, how to take it and how much, and what to do with us once we were flying. By focusing our attention on experiencing the different spirits in the sacred cave and concentrating on cutting the figures, we are now able to remember those events just like we would in our normal waking awareness."

Pondering what Marisol had just said, I absolutely had to agree. As I had mentioned before, my first experience with datura came when I was poisoned by a jealous Huichol man; I was immediately taken to the sacred ceremonial temple and was looked after by experienced shamans during my entire three-day flight when I flew to the land of Kieri and acquired my spirit-wolf allies. But my second experience with datura was completely different. Rafael had poisoned me, and since I had no experienced shamans or witches to help guide me, I basically went crazy, ended up unconscious in a taboo cave of the dead, and remembered absolutely nothing about what I did or how I got there. On my third flight with the datura, which was set up intentionally by my master teacher and curandero Don Vicente, I didn't remember everything, but I did remember the important parts that he set out for me to remember, just like my latest time with the witches Xilonen and Florinda.

Marisol agreed and added, "And I bet you those two guys that poisoned you used the *Datura inoxia* or other, more dangerous datura. Florinda gave you the *Datura stramonium*, and I bet that my father did too. Stramonium is, of course, still dangerous and even deadly, but with the guidance of an experienced witch, it can be more easily controlled."

With all these things coming to mind, I hadn't paid much attention to the fact that both Marisol and I were staring into the flowing creek the whole time we were remembering and talking. Simultaneously we took out our cut figures of the creek spirit.

"But of course!" Marisol exclaimed as she jumped from her seat. "Do you remember what Florinda said of the creek and other water spirits?"

"Water has memory," we both said at once.

Marisol continued, "Water is the solvent of the earth, a carrier of life."

"Whatever it touches becomes a part of its memory," I added.

"And whenever you're around it, you can use its flowing memory to remember things forgotten either intentionally or inadvertently," Marisol concluded as she held her figure so the sun behind us cast a squiggly shadow onto the water from the cut squiggle lines in the center of the figure.

At first, seeing the shadow on the water from Marisol's figure seemed perfectly appropriate for the moment. But as I stared at it, I had a strange feeling that something wasn't right. And then it hit me: I remembered what Florinda had said. "When the water spirit is present, the squiggly hole in the center will cast a shadow, not an image of light as it is supposed to in the normal world of light and dark. This is the sign that you have connected with the magical spirit of water."

Immediately I held my figure to make the shadows on the water through the holes of my figure. "Are you seeing what I'm seeing?" Marisol asked, noticing the startled look on my face.

"Yeah, I am. If that's not witchery, then I'm a toad. This defies every logical base of science that I've ever been taught."

"Me too," Marisol replied happily. "I guess the water spirit has shown itself to us. Let's go tell Florinda!"

———

Over the next two or three months, time seemed of no consequence in the secluded hacienda and the jungle and mountain areas surrounding it. Marisol and I, sometimes together and sometimes solo, explored the various spirit entities under the expert tutelage of Florinda. On some occasions, it would take me many excruciating days to make a connection with a certain spirit, but other spirits, in a similar manner to the creek spirit, revealed themselves to me almost immediately. Marisol found the same to be true, although it was very interesting that our experiences with certain spirits were so varied. Some that would come to her quickly I spent days on, and vice versa. For example, the butterfly spirit was very familiar to me through my connection with my Huichol shaman mentors who use the magical mariposas (butterflies) while acquiring certain visions, so the mariposa spirit came to me the very same day I went to find it. But Marisol spent nearly a week searching, stalking, waiting, and finally pleading to the spirit before it appeared and delivered its message to her at last. On the other hand, Marisol spent her first evening invoking one of the star spirits and acquired it immediately as a spirit ally that very first night, while I spent almost a week staring at it in the night sky, talking to it, even making promises to it before it finally revealed itself to me.

Once Marisol and I had each acquired all twenty of the spirit allies we had cut into figures in the cave, Florinda put on a grand party for us at the hacienda. It went without saying that the guests were all experienced curanderos and brujos who knew exactly what we were celebrating. Some of them I vaguely remembered seeing the night Don Julio dealt with his son in the alley in Veracruz City. Unfortunately, neither Don Vicente nor Xilonen nor anyone else I really knew was there. It occurred to me how few people I had actually interacted with while in the Tuxtlas. Except for a few witches, I really didn't know anyone. I had spent my time with witches and spirits in the jungle or in the house. If I wasn't so consumed by this world of the flying witches, I probably would have felt extremely lonely. But I didn't, and it was a festive party. The food, music, and dancing went on through most of the night.

Marisol, Florinda, and I were at the front door as the last of the guests were leaving and saying goodbye. There was much hugging and backslapping for Marisol and me for, as one witch put it, "getting our wings." But as one of the last guests approached me, I instinctively backed away with fright. I hadn't noticed him throughout the whole party, but he looked exactly like the "ghost" of Don Vicente's teacher who had given me the obsidian knife to kill the exit. He didn't say a word but slapped me hard in the back in a congratulatory way similar to what some of the other guests had done. However, his slap affected me profoundly, and my whole body began to shake. The man left without a word, and as I stood there I thought I might pass out. The worst thing was that neither Marisol nor Florinda seemed to even notice my condition, and I saw that neither of them said anything to the old man. It was as if they didn't even see him.

I ran to my room and, shaking and shivering in a cold sweat, sat on my bed. Ghostly shadows flew around the room. Some of them swooped down on me and I could feel their foul airs and even smell a few of them. It took me only seconds to realize that I was being attacked by evil spirits and that the old man had witched me. Somehow, I managed to keep my wits about me even though I was terrified as hell, and I reached under my bed and pulled out my box of paper spirit figures. Immediately I grabbed two protector spirits. In my right hand, I held Tlamocuitlahuijquetl, a powerful guardian of curanderos, and in my left I held up Teptl de Santa Rosa, the guardian spirit of the hills around the hacienda. Invoking both of the guardian spirits by calling their names, I could feel and see the shadow spirits instantly lose some of their power, and they no longer swooped directly at me. But somehow I knew that eventually they were powerful enough to win, and with that realization I became even more terrified of my situation.

Just then Florinda opened the door and rushed in. Seeing the evil spirits, she called them out by name and shouted for them to be gone, but they did not leave. "Someone has put a powerful curse on you, James," Florinda said to me calmly. "Now is the time to use the protection you worked so hard for. Bring forth your gall powder and place a little pile in each corner of your room, and place a little on your tongue."

I took out the powdered gall from my takwatsi and hurriedly did what Florinda prescribed. Within a few moments of placing the powders in the four corners and then some on my tongue, the evil spirits vanished from the room.

"That was a close call," Florinda said as we both sat down on my bed. "What in the world happened, and who attacked you?"

I proceeded to tell Florinda about the old man I had seen who had slapped me. At first, the look in her eyes told me that she was very concerned and afraid for me, because she indeed had not seen him, which to her meant that he was a master witch. But when I mentioned that he looked exactly like Don Vicente's dead teacher who had given me the obsidian knife in the graveyard, her grimace turned into a grin.

"Those old witches were testing you, James. Grab your things and meet us in the kitchen. I'll tell Marisol."

Florinda and Marisol were already in the kitchen when I got there. I noticed that they also had their things with them. "We are going on another journey for a few days, and we will leave right away," Florinda announced. "But first, James, you must go to the shrine of the hill spirit and thank him for helping you. You needn't leave any offerings this time, and you can leave your things here. Simply express your gratitude to the protector spirits and come back. Marisol will go with you, and on the way you can explain to her what just happened. We'll meet up again in the garden when you return."

As Marisol and I turned to leave, Florinda added, "And by the way, tell Don Julio that tonight we will fly to Mictlan, the cave of the dead."

———

flight of the ceratocaula

eading outside after putting on some shoes, Marisol and
I began walking a neatly maintained trail through the
jungle. I quickly explained to her what had happened in my
room, but I couldn't get out of my mind what Florinda had said
concerning Don Julio. What did he have to do with anything?
Even though I had no idea where the hacienda was actually
located in the vast Tuxtlas Mountains, it was clear that we were
nowhere near the city or Don Julio's house, and quite frankly
that felt very comforting, as I would be just as happy not to see
him.

"Florinda is connected to this place in a way that's hard to
fathom," Marisol said. "If she comments about giving someone
a message, then she must already know we are going to meet
them. Don't overanalyze it or you'll burst a brain cell."

And, of course, Marisol was completely right, because not
fifteen minutes later we encountered Don Julio in the jungle.

He had a canvas bag with him and was apparently collecting some medicinal plants for his practice. Upon coming up to him, I had a hard time even facing him after what had happened with Rafael—not that I blamed him for what he did but rather for just the complete oddness of the situation for me. I was not from the world of witches, and he was obviously one of the most powerful and influential witches in the world. Losing his son the way he did, and for me to have been involved, was very disconcerting. Plus, why in the world did we need to run into him out in the middle of the jungle?

Don Julio greeted us warmly as he puffed on a massive cigar that he seemed to be enjoying immensely. Marisol was about to deliver Florinda's message when Don Julio raised his hand to stop her, as if he already knew what she was going to say. He then reached into his bag and, with a piercing look, handed me my obsidian knife.

"This belongs to you, at least for now. I hope you won't need it tonight, but better safe than sorry."

He smiled as I took the knife, and then I saw that it was now tucked in a leather sheath that fit it perfectly and obviously had been handmade just for it. I bowed my head to Don Julio and quickly put the knife in my pocket, trying not to think of all the things it had done. I stared down at my feet for a few moments, not knowing what to say, and when I looked up, Don Julio was gone. Marisol simply shrugged her shoulders and continued walking up the path. The hill-spirit shrine was not far, and after saying my thanks we went and met up with Florinda in the garden.

"I was planning to give you guys a few days' rest, but now it seems that things have changed," Florinda said casually as we sat on benches in the midst of all the outrageous flowers of datura and brugmansia and whatever else was growing that I had no knowledge of.

"Don Vicente sent us a powerful test by having his teacher attack James with those evil spirits. But, of course, he knew you had protection, so you weren't in any serious danger unless you simply let fear overcome you, which you didn't. That was the real test, because he knows that the next and most dangerous part of your training and of Marisol's is about to begin. I believe he didn't bother testing Marisol because he knew his daughter already obtained the gall with me many years ago, and she has grown up in the world of witches.

"It is important for you to realize that all of the spirits you have been working with and learning about the last few months are 'good' spirits. They are the spirits that nurture, protect, and give life. But now it's time for you to learn about the other kinds of spirits, the kinds that make beings sick, conjure bad fortune, and kill. But let me be clear: these spirits are not evil unto themselves. Death is not evil, just as sickness is not evil; they are both simply situations of life. The reason that some of these spirits are called evil is because witches with wrong intent use them to harm for their own gain, and *that* is evil."

Rising from the bench, Florinda motioned for us to follow her, and we walked to an area under a large arch that, for whatever reason, I hadn't seen yet. Passing under the shadow of the arch, I experienced a kind of sensory overload from a combination of bright sunlight, bright white flowers, the sound of running water, and an incredibly sweet, flowery scent.

Laughing joyfully at my reaction, Florinda said, "Welcome to the home of our dear ceratocaula, *nexehuac*, or, in Spanish, *torna loco* (makes you crazy). With the spirit of the ceratocaula, we will fly to the place where we can capture and tame some evil spirits."

Knowing by now that Florinda meant full well what she said, I temporarily bypassed the significance of her words and instead focused my intention on the plants. This was the first species of datura I had seen actually growing in water, and it seemed to absolutely love it. They were extremely healthy, vibrant, and beautiful. Plus, unlike the *Datura inoxia*, whose smell made me want to vomit every time I touched one, the ceratocaula had fragrant flowers that were almost intoxicating by themselves. And the flowers were amazing. They were large for a datura, but the amazing part was the coloring. Basically, they were white, like many other datura, but these funnel-shaped flowers upon closer inspection were faintly pinkish-violet inside, and if you looked at them kind of out of the corner of your eyes, the outside radiated a bluish tone that felt rather eerie for some reason. However, of all the oddities of this datura, the one that struck me the most was the seedpod out of which the flying potion would be made. The ceratocaula was the only datura I had ever seen that did not have seedpods full of spines that basically yelled out to you "don't eat me." The ceratocaula seedpods were completely smooth and resembled the shape and smoothness of an egg. Although the ceratocaula pods didn't yell "eat me," they certainly didn't discourage animals or humans from eating them like the other datura species did.

Florinda instructed Marisol and me to collect five seedpods each and to thank the plants for their gifts, which we did. Once that was done, we all went back into the house, grabbed our things, and went out the side doors to the walled courtyard of the fire pit. A solemn mood had overtaken our group, and at this point I wasn't even surprised to see a nice fire crackling, even though there appeared to be no one around who could have made it.

Florinda added to the solemn mood by asking us, "Do you know where ceratocaula got its name?"

"Yeah, I do," Marisol replied while staring into the fire. "My father told me once, and I never forgot what he said. He told me that *ceratocaulus* means 'stalk like a horn' in Latin. Most people think that it was botanically named that because the stems grow differently than other daturas—they don't fork off as much but instead they curve like a horn. But father said the deeper significance was that witches who ingested it could more easily summon wicked beasts with horns from the underworld that were equated with the horned devil of the Catholics."

"Very good, little curandera," Florinda replied in more light-hearted voice, as if somehow the worst had now been said. "And why would we want to summon such beasts from the under-world?"

Memories flooded my mind of the evil shadows that had attacked me earlier, and an unfamiliar feeling of vengeance came over me as I said harshly, "So we can capture them and make them our slaves."

Florinda laughed. "Well, 'slaves' may be a little strong, but you have the right idea. It is not enough to simply have protection from these beings. Our spirit guides and guardians can only do so much. The only way to properly cure someone that has been witched by evil spirits is to be able to call those spirits and have them actually come to you so you can deal with them, kind of like a dog who knows it has done something wrong but when you catch it doing it, it will still come to you when called because you are its master. And, like a dog, there is no guarantee that the dog won't do the bad thing again, but at least you stopped it from doing whatever it was doing wrong because it knew to listen to you and respected you. When evil spirits are sent to harm people by evil witches, we need to know those spirits and have them obey us so we can stop them from doing what they are doing. Like a dog with sharp teeth and claws, fighting with an evil spirit is a last option. The much better option is to have the dog, or the evil spirit, stop what it's doing without fighting.

"But these spirits are not like domesticated dogs that will listen or be trained. They are like jackals and cannot be completely tamed. The best you can do with jackals is scare them off, and once they get to know you and fear you as they would a lion, they will back off more quickly."

As Florinda was speaking about evil spirits, my head became full of doubts. I wondered if I would actually be able to see them or do anything about them, or if I wanted to, or if they even existed. It was one thing to see and tangibly feel the spirit of a stream or mountain, an animal or a tree. I had been doing that without even knowing it since I was a small child playing in the woods. But except for my time in Veracruz with the witches, I don't remember ever having actually seen or felt an evil spirit. Sure, I had experienced firsthand the death of my father from cancer and had known friends and relatives killed by disease, accidents, crime, and even war. But were these seemingly bad events caused by spirits? I was having reservations believing that.

"This is not a matter of faith or belief, James," Florinda said, as if reading my mind. "This concerns tangible energy and forces that can be manipulated and even directed by evil people. As I said, death and sickness are not evil; they are simply facts of life. However, intentional murder, rape, or torture among human beings is the result of imbalance. We can call these imbalances *spirits* because we have no other name for them. But they can be named and they do exist. We as curanderos are not always responsible, required, or even invited to correct these imbalances. Some things are simply meant to be. The most important thing for us is to be able to help when we are asked. That is the job we have been given in this lifetime. Especially when someone has hired an evil witch to cause harm to another or a person has become so wicked that he or she preys on the innocent or takes more than is needed.

"Right now, it's best if you simply concentrate on meeting and establishing some kind of control over these forces, even if that is simply to make them run from you. Once you have acquired their figures, you will be ready to learn how to use that knowledge in the helping of others. That will be the next and final part of your formal training. Right now we have an appointment for both of you to meet some spirits."

Florinda prepared the grate and pot on the fire while Marisol and I cut open the seedpods and crushed them with the mortar and pestle. Florinda told us that she was going to make a much stronger mixture this time because we would be administering the spirit of the ceratocaula into our dreaming bodies in a different way.

Marisol and I put the ground ceratocaula into the pot, and I saw that Florinda had put less than half of the sacred corn beverage into the mix with it this time. She continued by saying, "In the case of both the ceratocaula and the spirits we are going to meet, we don't want to fully open ourselves to them. The ceratocaula is the trickiest of all the daturas and will surely attempt to trick or delude us if we are not careful and do not take the appropriate measures to avoid her gaining complete control. Her fragrance, her beautiful flowers, and her egg-shaped pods are all disguises she wears to lure people, animals, and even spirits into her games. That is why she is the best datura to use in order to meet the lying, cheating, and malicious spirits of the underworld."

This time Florinda used a simple wooden spoon to stir the cauldron. "With the stramonium we can open to its power by allowing it to enter into the mystical power point of our body: our genital region. But with the ceratocaula, we will allow it to enter only on the outside of our body, through our skin and not any of our mucous membranes." Taking the cauldron off the fire, she continued, "This is both symbolic and practical. Symbolically we want to show the ceratocaula spirit that we would like to fly with her, but that is all. We are making it very clear that we are not seeking some sort of intimate relationship. And on a purely practical level, it is much easier to regulate and be sure of the proper amount to use of this dangerous spirit if we gradually apply her essence."

Florinda produced two more spoons and, placing the pot between us, she instructed us to apply the gooey mixture as she was doing. First we smeared some around both our ankles, then on the inside of our wrists, then on the center of our chest, and finally on the forehead. "Once you start to feel slightly drowsy, then follow the same procedure again," she instructed.

I was so pumped with adrenaline I kind of laughed to myself that it would take a heck of a lot more than a few smears of paste, more like an elephant tranquilizer, to get me sleepy after all we had just spoken about and the thoughts of challenging a bunch of evil spirits. But, of course, being the skilled witch she was, Florinda accurately predicted the sleepy feeling I began to feel after about half an hour or so. I was actually the first one of us to reapply the paste, but soon after so did Marisol and Florinda.

"The next phase will be the feeling of a strong wind rushing over your whole body and soul. When you get to the point of feeling that the wind is so strong that it's going to carry you away and you cannot hang on much longer, quickly reapply another coating of paste and then lean back and let the wind take you."

By the time I had put my second coating on, I was really feeling the affects of the ceratocaula, and Florinda's voice seemed far away. But I didn't feel any wind, so I kept staring intently into the fire. A few minutes later, it hit me: a single strong gust that lasted only a few seconds but that almost knocked me over. Recovering and wrongly thinking that would be it, another strong blast hit me, but this time it lasted more than a full minute, and in order to not be blown away, I hurled myself onto the ground and rode it out.

I knew that another gust was inevitably coming and this time I would surely be blown away. Looking over at Florinda, she simply smiled, and I could hear in my mind, "Hurry and put on the last coat of paste, then lie back down and relax. Whatever you do, be sure to concentrate on the cave of the dead. We will meet there in Mictlan. You have been there before, so you should be able to easily fly there. DO NOT let your mind wander or who knows where you'll end up."

Quickly I put the paste on my body parts and just before lying down I looked over at Marisol, but she was already gone. Within seconds, a huge gust of air came once more, and I simply let myself be taken. Interestingly, once I was "flying," the wind seemed normal albeit purposeful and not threatening at all. Everything around me was dark and obscure, but as I gradually got used to it, I could make out features in the landscape below me. The sensation, both visually and with all my other senses, was that I was actually flying high above the mountains of the jungle.

Hearing Florinda's voice in my ear, I remembered to conjure up the image and feeling of the cave of Mictlan, and immediately it felt like I had changed course. Then something truly odd happened: I felt a tug from someone pulling me off my course, and I felt myself resisting the pull. Again I focused my attention on Mictlan, but immediately I heard a strange female voice in my head say, "Dear boy, why would you want to go to such a dreadful place? You can fly! You can go anywhere you want! In this world or many others! Come, let me guide you!"

Admittedly, I listened to the voice and for a split second thought about the endless possibilities. But I also had enough experience in the witches' world to know without question that my life depended on meeting Florinda and Marisol in Mictlan. From somewhere deep inside me I blurted out, "Nice try, Ceratocaula, you trickster!"

And the next thing I knew, I was standing with my traveling partners at the entrance to the cave.

———

mictlan and tlalocan

"Well done!" Florinda said. She and Marisol were both laughing.

"We both heard you yelling at Ceratocaula. I guess she likes men, because she didn't even try to take me," Marisol added cheerfully.

But as I turned to look at the black entrance to the cave, I suddenly did not feel cheery at all.

"Torch!" Florinda commanded loudly, and a huge torch of fire appeared in her hand.

"Torch!" Marisol commanded, with a similar result.

"Torch!" I commanded, but absolutely nothing happened.

Marisol chuckled, but Florinda said, "Don't worry, James, it takes practice. We really only need one torch anyway. Come on, let's go in."

"Showoff!" I whispered to Marisol as I followed closely in her footsteps.

The interior of the cave, as well as the awful stench, was exactly as I remembered it. The first time I flew there, I was completely out of control and had no memory of how I got there. This time I had flown there with intention, and although I was still somewhat apprehensive, I felt like I was in total control. Florinda glanced back at me with a nod, as she, of course, had heard my thoughts.

We walked much deeper into the cave than I had been before, and there were passages running off on both sides giving me the distinct impression that it would be supremely easy to get lost. Florinda seemed to know exactly where she was going, and after descending a long flight of stone stairs we arrived at a fairly large chamber that seemed to have four passages leading into it; the stairs we had just come down and then three other tunnels coming in at 90-degree angles to one another. Intuitively I knew that all four passages were aligned with the cardinal directions, but I wasn't sure which of the directions we had entered from.

As Florinda and Marisol showed their torches around, I thought I saw a figure that might have been a person scurry away, but I wasn't sure. What I was sure of was where the horrific stench was coming from. We had found it, and it made me catch my breath. I had been here before. Xilonen and the Huichol dreamer Alberto had taught me the basics of navigating the underworld in my dreams, and this was the center of the underworld. But two things I realized right away. First of all, I had never felt as aware when I was here in my dreams before, and second, the place was not nearly complete.

There should have been great temple here in the center, called Tlalocan, and a city surrounding it. Instead, in front of us was only the altar that was usually in the center of the temple. Even though everything else seemed to be missing, I remembered the altar as being exactly the same. It was a low altar of stone maybe twenty feet across and four feet wide in the center of the room, and it was covered with offerings both ancient and recent. Most of the offerings looked like the remains of animals that probably had been sacrificed, but there were also human skulls and other bones that looked human. In addition, there were the remains of hundreds, if not thousands, of candles, amulets, and effigies of all kinds of beings, including human dolls and paper-cut figures. The place was truly disturbing in that it simply exuded intentional malice and deliberate chaos in the same measure that a beautiful church can exude supreme morality and order.

"It's all here, James," Florinda said as she read my thoughts. "You just can't see it because you flew here a different way this time. This time we are here by way of the ceratocaula, and so most, if not all, of the good things in the underworld will not shine through. We are here on a mission to discover some of the mysteries of the evil side of the underworld, so with that intention, that is what we will encounter. But, as you know, the underworld is also filled with great joy and light. On this flight, we journey on the truly dark side. Let's begin right away and call the spirit that guards and sends us this awful stench. I think I saw him running from us when we entered.

"Hey Tlasoli, wind—come over here and show yourself!" Florinda commanded.

Hastily Florinda handed me her torch and instructed us to light the torches that were stuck into holes above each of the four entrances to Tlalocan. With that done and the cave eerily illuminated, it was now clear that it was much larger than it had first appeared. Next to the huge altar was a kind of work area that was actually fairly free of debris or refuse. With a nod and knowing that we understood what she wanted, Marisol and I went to the stone table, where I guessed thousands upon thousands of figures, dolls, amulets, and who knows what else had been created. Taking out our paper and razors, we stood intently waiting.

Florinda, however, was not so patient. "You filthy vermin, I told you to show yourself. Or would you prefer I send you to guard a garbage dump in Mexico City?"

Immediately a shadowy figure appeared near the entrance we had entered through.

"Before you cut the figure of this disgusting being that feeds on the stench of rotting flesh and disease, put two pieces of paper together so that you can cut two figures at once."

Marisol and I both cut the figure of the shadowy image on the wall, and then Florinda told us to each burn one of our copies in the flame of a torch and keep one so that we would remember this hideous but important spirit.

With one copy of each of our effigies burned, a nice brisk-smelling breeze blew through the cave and the shadow of Tlasoli vanished. Thankfully the god-awful smell of the place somehow went with him.

"He'll of course be back again when he collects himself, just like most spirits, but at least for now we got rid of him,"

Florinda sighed. "And although he is a minor character, he is important, because many little witches like the brujos pequeños can call and control evil winds such as Tlasoli, so it is good for you to know them, too, as they can cause suffering to those that have been cursed by them.

"Now before we call the real dangerous spirits, those such as a brujo negro or brujo de muerte would use, I want you both to cast a circle of your gall powder on the ground around you for protection. And get ready, for you are about to meet some of the most malicious spirits that exist in the current reality of human beings.

"The gall will protect you," Florinda continued while we sprinkled the powder on the ground, "by not allowing the spirit to permanently attach itself to you, but it will not protect you from feeling the spirit. This means that you will have to battle with it to get it off of you. There are three things I want you to do after I call each spirit. First, I want you to see and feel the spirit. This will be extremely difficult, but just remember that whatever you feel or whatever the spirit does to you, it is not happening to you in the physical world. Because you are traveling with the ceratocaula right now, you will probably feel the effects of the spirits as though this was happening to your physical body, but it is not. It is necessary for you to feel the spirit, but the ceratocaula allows you to feel without anything happening to you physically; this is a battle of the soul, so when you are ready I want you to simply expel the spirit from you as you would simply cast off a robe or a pair of shoes. Then I want you to cut the figure of the spirit in paper so you will clearly remember it when we get back."

I had a hundred questions to ask, but Florinda didn't allow me even one as she immediately faced one of the cave openings and commanded, "Evil spirit of Tonallan, come to the altar of Tlalocan and show yourself."

Almost immediately a wind came from the tunnel and flickered all the torches as it entered the main cave. The shadow it produced was elusive and wispy, like it was afraid to be seen. I had never experienced a shadow from a spirit like it before. I knew from my previous dream experiences with the Aztec underworld that Tonallan was in the west, but I didn't know specifically what spirit Florinda had summoned. It occurred to me that maybe she didn't know either, because she did not call the spirit by name.

As if drawn like a magnet, the spirit immediately came at us, but when it hit the circle of gall powder it shrieked. The powder definitely slowed it down, but it continued forward relentlessly until it grabbed hold of me and threw me to the ground. I was so shocked by the flood of feelings and emotions I was suddenly experiencing that I was completely immobilized. The spirit had an iron grip and was holding me down tight. I could feel the burning desire of the spirit to have me, to foul me, to invade me. It had an uncontrollable lust to force itself on me, and then I finally realized what the spirit was. The spirit was Rape.

Knowing now what the spirit wanted, I struggled as hard as I could, but it was no use. It was so strong that I was powerless over it. In horror, I felt it enter and invade me against my will. It was one of the most intensely repulsive feelings I had ever experienced. And the spirit kept it coming until I was totally spent and struggled no longer.

Upon completely breaking my will, the spirit finished with me and backed off. I had intense feelings of shame for what I had just allowed to be done to me. I felt dirty and somehow guilty of something. Violated and angry, I cursed at the spirit, but then I remembered Florinda's words. This was happening in a dream trance, so nothing physical had really happened to me. It was up to me not to let this malicious spirit affect me, so I yelled at it with all my soul, "Begone, evil spirit! I will not let you give me your filthy, shameful guilt. You have no power over me. Begone!"

My force of will prevailed, and the spirit evaporated into space. I quickly cut my paper effigy of the spirit and put it into my case. Marisol was lying on the ground immobilized, and when I looked over to Florinda, I could hear her thoughts telling me that the spirit still had her. Marisol was in some ways stronger than me and was still fighting to not let the spirit break her. I wanted desperately to help her, but I could feel Florinda telling me no.

Eventually Marisol rose and immediately cut her figure of the spirit and placed it in her case. Florinda wasted no time and, facing the southern opening, she yelled, "Foul spirit of Atotonican, I command you here to the altar of Tlalocan!"

The spirit that the wind from the south brought was completely different from the west. This shadow seemed to almost be on fire as it entered the cave and flew right at us. When it hit the circle of gall, it turned into a wall of whitish stone, and

I thought I heard it laugh. I sighed in relief that it did not penetrate our defense and did not touch me. But just then it burst into flames, and the rock wall transformed into a giant mirror. I became afraid. I knew then that this spirit was Fear. But the spirit did not simply mirror physical fear, such as falling from a cliff or drowning; somehow it knew that would not affect me very much. I guess everyone feels and deals with their fears differently, and the spirit knew exactly what I was most afraid of. More deeply than I've ever felt before, the spirit mirrored back to me my fears of dying alone, of loneliness and abandonment, of being hurt or betrayed by someone I truly loved, of inadequacy and failure. I felt the complete dissolution of my resolve.

The spirit did not need to touch me in order to mirror and amplify my feelings back at me. I felt them each as strongly as if daggers were being thrust into my heart. Instead of feeling ashamed, like I had at being raped, this time I simply felt like a coward, and that felt almost equally as bad. In fact, this spirit affected me even stronger. I suddenly realized that I was wallowing in fears to the point where I was actually shrinking and the spirit would eventually consume me. But I didn't know what to do—I felt powerless over being exposed to my deepest fears, and I was fading fast. It was a true disintegration of the soul.

Just before I felt as if the spirit would crush me into a tiny pile of sand, I saw the image of Itzamna the dwarf king in my mind, and I remembered what he had told me the very first time we met. He had explained to me that the world was full of magic, and with that magic our thoughts, feelings, and emotions create the reality we live in, so in every moment we need to be conscious about our thoughts and actions. It was the awareness that our thoughts and actions affect not only ourselves but everything around us. I was feeding the spirit and making it stronger by succumbing to my feelings of fear.

With that realization, I looked deeply into the mirror and cast it away. Immediately I cut the spirit's figure and put it in my case. Marisol was waiting for me this time, and she smiled at me as Florinda turned to the east and called to the direction of Apan.

The spirit that rode on the wind from Apan smelled like the ocean and was sticky like a hot, humid day. It passed right through the circle of gall and engulfed me just like a wave in the ocean. In fact, I experienced a very similar sensation to being effortlessly taken underwater by a giant wave. The impact of this wave was so strong, I knew that I was in for a real fight for life. Desperately looking around me as I reeled out of control from the impact of the wave, everything seemed murky and dark as if I were physically under the water in the ocean. When I finally stopped being tossed and turned, my only thought was to "swim" to the light of the torch I could vaguely see as a pinprick of light above me.

As I began to try and swim upward, I suddenly realized I would never make it; it was way too far. Panic hit me, and just as had happened to me in the past during other near-death experiences, I began to see my life flash before my eyes. That's when I knew what the spirit was. It was the stealer of souls, and it was taking mine.

A feeling of melancholy overtook me as I felt my memories of the past and my hopes and dreams for the future being drained from me in my futile attempt to swim toward the light in this cosmic ocean. The pinprick of light above me was only a mirage of hope; there was no hope for me. This time I had truly lost to the evil spirit. There was little left of my soul inside of me, and I slipped into the darkness of a deep coma.

At some distant and faraway level of consciousness, I somehow knew that I was not dead—that was not what the spirit wanted. The spirit wanted my soul, not my life. It was the most excruciating torture of them all, knowing that you are not dead but lacking the ability to live. If there was such a thing as hell, this would be it.

My savior came as a hand and arm reached down into the cosmic water from the pinprick of light and pulled me to the surface. It was Florinda, and she helped me stand up and brushed me off. Marisol was cutting her figure, and I looked up at Florinda in disbelief that I was actually back. I wanted to ask her about what had happened, but as I caught her eye, I knew instantly. She had summoned the spirit to steal my soul so that I would truly experience what it feels like for a healer to bring back a person's soul that had been taken or lost.

I cut my figure of the soul-stealer spirit, and Marisol and I faced the last entrance, Mictan, the entrance to the north. Neither of us had any doubt what the wind would bring us this time. We also had no idea what we would do.

Florinda called to the north, and a strong breeze entered the cave. It was cold as ice, and the shadow was large and heavy and opaque. It came to mind that this spirit, unlike all the others, was exactly what I expected it to be. It felt malicious and bloodthirsty and cruel and indifferent to life. But compared to the three other spirits, I actually felt let down by this one. It seemed so predictable, and even though it might be a tough fight, I felt completely confident that I would defeat it. The spirit, of course, was Death, but I knew it wasn't my time yet.

Then Death swiftly reached out and grabbed my neck, and I knew I was in trouble. If Death wanted me, it could snuff me out in a second or it could make me suffer painfully before it took me. I was completely at its mercy, but I also wasn't willing to just give up. Don Julio suddenly popped into my head, and since my hands were free, I easily got out my obsidian knife and stabbed Death with all my might.

To my surprise, the spirit actually let me go and slowly backed off as I thought to myself, "Well, that wasn't too difficult."

As I put my knife back in its sheath, strong arms grabbed me from behind and I felt the cold, hard edge of a blade slice open my throat and warm blood run down my neck. Thrown to the ground, I turned and looked up as I frantically grabbed my throat with my hands, but I knew it was no use. The lesson of the spirit of the north was not simply death for me. It was murder.

With my last few breaths, I fully felt the hate of the spirit and the viciousness with which it had attacked me. I felt cheated and resentful of the spirit. I wanted to kill it before I died, but I knew I couldn't, and that made me mad. I wondered why it had murdered me—what were the motives or passions behind this act of murder? I had to know. I wasn't going to simply die for nothing and without knowing.

In my final seconds, I summoned up all my will and pulled the spirit into me. And I finally understood. The spirit of Murder was a reaction that, at the moment of murder, the murderer had absolutely no control over. Whatever the reasons for the murder, in the moment of the murder, the murderer felt completely justified in the action.

As soon as I truly felt the spirit of Murder, I felt pity. It was not mercy or forgiveness but only pity at the fact that a human being could get to a point of having a reason to murder another person. The spirit of Murder that was inside me was not premeditated killing like an animal does for food. This spirit of Murder was induced by a situation, a feeling, or an emotion, not simply the need for food. And that was just sad and heartbreaking.

Everyone has his or her own personal feelings about love and hate, fear and death, murder and rape, and why people do hurtful things to each other. And I guess what the spirits in Tlalocan taught me that day was what I needed to know at that time and place.

I cut my figure of Murder and put it in my box with the others.

———

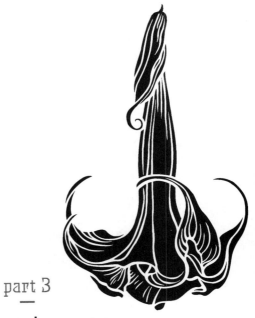

part 3
—
dream-trance
healing

the greedy politician

he moment we entered the house I could feel the vacuum of the Ehecacihuauh, one of the soul-stealing spirits. We were escorted through the lavish mansion and into the study, where Mr. Rodriguez was sitting behind his desk and his wife was seated in the corner, waiting for us. The feelings of intense pain, loss, and helplessness pervaded the study even though Mr. Rodriguez and his wife externally projected the façade of control appropriate to their social and political standing. As Mr. Rodriguez rose from his chair to greet us, I looked over at Marisol at the same time she looked at me and, catching each other's eye, we silently acknowledged the beginning of our first case as publicly known tetlachihuics.

Don Vicente had sent us to the city after receiving a request for help from Mayor Rodriguez. The day before, Marisol and I had been summoned to Don Vicente's office, where he had proceeded to inform us that we were ready to begin replacing him and the other older generation of tetlachihuics. For many months, I had been continuing my training in dream trance with Don Vicente by seeing his clients with him and further learning his art, as Marisol had also been doing with Florinda. So after having passed through the many tests and challenges of acquiring spirit allies, learning about the pantheon of spirits and how to fly in the underworld to acquire information pertinent to the everyday world, and being assistant to hundreds of healing sessions with our teachers, Marisol and I were in the city of Veracruz on the recommendation of Marisol's father to help in the case of the kidnapping of the mayor's daughter. We were instructed to go and meet with the mayor and his wife and basically find out all we could about what had happened and then come back to Don Vicente's place in Catemaco and decide what to do.

But from the very first moment that Mayor Rodriguez opened his mouth, I knew for sure that there was much more going on than just the kidnapping of his daughter. It was just all too simple. It didn't take a Sherlock Holmes to see that the luxuriant lifestyle of the mayor went hand in hand with the notorious corruption of Mexican politics. The fact that Mexican police and government were so corrupt was so taken for granted that police and politicians didn't even bother covering it up anymore. And that the mayor's daughter went for a jog and was kidnapped went way beyond Mr. Rodriguez simply being the mayor.

It was clear that while both Mr. and Mrs. Rodriguez loved their only daughter with all their hearts, it became apparent within only a few minutes that they weren't going to tell us anything more about the situation than we already knew. And that's precisely why the mayor had originally called Don Vicente. He knew that if Don Vicente, a well-known witch-doctor, could find his daughter, then his reputation with his colleagues and the rest of the shady and corrupt organizations he dealt with would remain intact and he wouldn't be perceived as a squealer or a snitch. In his position, this was a perfectly legitimate course of action. For centuries people have been blaming witchcraft or seeking the help of witches in order to hide or distort the truth of actual situations that have nothing to do with the supernatural. By turning to witches, Mayor Rodriguez was taking the easy way out, because whether he or the police or Marisol and I were to find his daughter or not, the result would now still be seen as the consequence of the influence of witches. This was a good thing for the mayor but not so good for Marisol and me, or the daughter, because we would not be given any more information than she was simply snatched up while out jogging in the park.

Marisol could see that I was clearly frustrated, but, having dealt with corrupt officials her whole life, she took the lead and asked if we could spend some time in the daughter, Regina's, room, since speaking with the mayor and his wife was getting us nowhere. As we were escorted by a servant to Regina's room, I couldn't help but feel sorry for the Rodriguezes. For as affluent and successful as they were, they had got themselves into the position of gambling with their daughter's life instead of telling us the truth, and that fact was stealing both of their souls to a much greater extent than even the physical or emotional loss of Regina to their family.

We stayed in Regina's room for almost two hours, getting the feel for her energy and soul. Marisol was extremely happy because she felt that Regina's room really did feel like her and was not the sterilized living space of many wealthy children. I agreed. Regina seemed like an ordinary teenage girl, with posters and pictures on the walls and various kinds of clothes, shoes, music, and DVDs.

Done with her room and wanting to visit the park where she was supposedly abducted, we were ready to leave the house when the mayor told us that he had received a phone call while we were in Regina's room. It was from the kidnappers, and they had made a ransom demand. The mayor also informed us that the federal police had now been called in and that they had a special task force for these kinds of kidnappings. Even though it was common knowledge, the mayor insisted on giving us a detailed account of the increase in these types of kidnappings across the country and the need for special police units that handled these cases. What the mayor left out, and what we all knew, was that there was also an increase in hostage deaths even when the kidnappers were paid and the federal police or private professional negotiators had brokered the deal. There was not much honor left among thieves or kidnappers in Mexico, and we all knew it.

I was not surprised that as we were leaving the house the *federales* arrived, and so they all saw us leaving. Of course, they had no idea who I was, but more than a few of them would probably know who Marisol and her father were. The timing of their arrival with our departure definitely felt like more than a coincidence, and when I commented on that to Marisol she silently nodded her head up and down in dismayed agreement.

We went to the nearby park and walked around, but neither of us felt or found anything about Regina that would help us, so we drove the three hours back to Catemaco to consult with Don Vicente.

He was not the least surprised by anything we told him about what had happened, but I was completely surprised by Marisol. Without me or anyone else noticing, Marisol had successfully acquired items from the three main people involved in the case so far. She brought forth from her pockets things from Regina, the mayor, and his wife, which she laid on the table. Don Vicente laughed with glee at my surprise and said, "My little one here cannot only transform her appearance and walk right by you without you even knowing, but she can also pick your pocket even when she's in plain sight."

Somehow Marisol had obtained the mayor's pocket watch, some hairs from the shoulder of Regina's mother's dress, and a set of earrings and a handwritten note from Regina's room. When Don Vicente saw the pocket watch he roared with laughter once again, and when he finally calmed down enough for me to ask him what was so funny, he simply, in a mockingly serious voice, told me that without a doubt the mayor would know who had taken it, but he would never ask for it back, no matter how much it meant to him or what it had cost. If a tetla-chihuic has a reason to take something from you, you can consider it gone for good. "Mayor Rodriguez is peeing his pants right now knowing that we have his watch. And he's probably searching frantically for anything else that might be missing,"

Don Vicente added with pride as he looked lovingly at his very capable witch-daughter.

After Don Vicente heard all we had to say, he recommended that I take the mayor's watch and dream with it, and that Marisol take Regina's things and dream with them. His impression was that the mayor's wife had little or nothing to do with the actual situation, and that unfortunately for her she was simply along for the ride.

Marisol drove out to the hacienda to do her dream work in her room, and I went to my dreaming room in Don Vicente's house. Following my normal routine, I lit my candle and stared deeply into the flowing flame until I could shut my eyes and still see the flame. I never asked how Marisol got into her dream-trance state, but for me the easiest and quickest way was with a flame in complete silence and darkness.

One of the most distinct differences in my dream trance after having worked with Florinda and the various daturas was the speed in which I could reach that state. And almost always I felt a wind similar to the time with the ceratocaula that would take me flying into the underworld. In contrast, Marisol once mentioned to me that when she flew to the underworld, she had the sensation of being pulled or sucked in, but she had no sensation of wind.

Clutching the mayor's watch and not sure exactly where to go, I flew to the center of Tlalocan and landed at the front steps of the great temple. Unexpectedly I was in a great sea of people. There was something major happening at the temple, and as far as the eye could see there were people standing outside the temple, seemingly waiting for something important to happen.

I looked around frantically for some clue as to what to do, and within seconds I felt a sharp pain in my shin as if someone had just kicked me.

I looked down, and there was my good friend Itzamna, the dwarf king. I smiled at him and was about to give him a big hug when he threw his arms in the air and in a scolding voice said, "About time you got here, boy! Where have you been? There's little time left! Come on!"

In my condor form, I flew over the great mass of people and saw why everyone was gathered. Set in the middle of the courtyard in front of the temple was a giant raised platform with a sacrificial altar. There were many Aztec priests on the stage, and with horror I noticed only one woman: Regina. I recognized her from the photos I had seen of her, but now she was dressed in a white gown and I knew immediately that she was the one meant to be sacrificed. I landed on the corner of the platform to see the head priest lead Regina to the altar. The head priest was Mayor Rodriguez, her own father, and next to the stone altar was a hooded priest with a sickle-shaped ax in his hands.

It didn't take a rocket scientist to figure out what was going to happen next, but I sure as hell wasn't going to let it happen. Imagine, a father who would kill his own daughter—not on my watch! I sprang up, intending to gouge the mayor's eyes out, but something caught me and dragged me down. It was Itzamna.

"You are only here as a witness, my friend," Itzamna said urgently. "We must let this unfold naturally and without interference."

I couldn't believe what Itzamna was saying. I had to save the girl. Why else would I be there? What was the point in me watching her die?

But that's exactly what I did. Both Itzamna and I stood there and watched the mayor hand his daughter over to the executioner, who promptly detached her head from her body.

———

My eyes shot open, and I ran to find Don Vicente. He was already waiting outside my dreaming room, and he grabbed me strongly but kindly and settled me down. We went back into my dreaming room, and I told my dream to my teacher. He asked only one question: "Did the mayor actually see his daughter die?"

Remembering back to my dream, I clearly remembered the mayor turning and walking away after he gave his daughter to the executioner, so I was fairly sure he didn't watch it actually happen.

Don Vicente grinned and told me I had done a good job, and that I should go to my bedroom and get some rest. Marisol would come in the morning with her dream, and we would decide what to do then.

Marisol's dream was not as graphic as mine, but it also held much significance. In her dream trance, Marisol saw two extremely pertinent things. First, she saw Regina with a woman dressed in a black-hooded cloak taking her away to a dark place. Next, Regina was in a field of large plants and surrounded by evil men who were watching her. But the best thing was that even though Regina was being held captive by these men, Marisol believed without a shadow of a doubt that she was still alive. Don Vicente asked Marisol and I to interpret the dreams together.

I began, "It seems clear to me that the mayor knew about the kidnapping."

"I agree," said Marisol. "It seems that he knowingly did something that might get her killed."

"But, I think, the beheading I saw was simply the mayor's subconscious manifesting the loss of Regina and not her actual death, and that he really doesn't know where she is," I added.

"Yes. But you did see him hand her over to the executioner, so he is somehow responsible. I think that the woman in black in my dream is a witch. So how and why did she take Regina?"

"*The mayor made a deal with the witch!*" Marisol and I both shouted out triumphantly at the same time.

"Very good," Don Vicente commented, "but where is the girl?"

Neither Marisol nor I could discern that from Marisol's dream, so we decided to confront Mr. Rodriguez with what we now knew.

Don Vicente called the mayor to tell him that we were coming and to expect us, but told him nothing more.

On the way back to the city, Marisol and I racked our brains trying to figure out why she had seen Regina in a field being guarded by men, but the answer eluded us as to where or why she had that vision.

The mayor was alone in his study when we arrived, and immediately Marisol confronted him.

"We know you made some sort of a deal with a witch that included your daughter. If you ever want to see her again, you had better tell us exactly what happened."

A shocked look came over the man's face like he was in no way expecting we would find that out. "How in the hell do you know that?" he said angrily once he had regained his composure. "Are you witches in league with her?"

"Hardly," I said in mocking tone. "Look, Mayor, we aren't going to judge you for what you did. What's done is done. But you can't lie to us. We will eventually find out the truth. So why don't you just tell us what you did?"

"I don't even believe in witchcraft," the mayor said, "but I was desperate. I was going to lose the election last year, and I didn't know what to do. So my assistant talked me into seeing a witch, and the witch promised to help me. But she could see how desperate I was, and she made me agree that if she used a spell that got me elected, she would take the soul of my daughter. That was the price. The only reason I agreed was because I didn't believe she could actually do it—I was simply grasping at straws. This is crazy. I still can't believe this is happening."

"So the phone call from the kidnappers was a lie," Marisol said.

"Yes."

"And the abduction?" I asked.

"Regina went to bed that night, and in the morning she was gone."

"Tell us how to find the witch," Marisol demanded.

The door to the witch's office was open, and a few moments after we entered she came out from behind a curtain that served as the back wall. She was a homely looking woman dressed in an elegant black dress, with many necklaces of symbols and talismans. When she first walked in she exuded confidence and had an air of superiority about her. But after she took one look at Marisol, and then at me, I could tell that the thought crossed her mind to run out the back door. This witch had at least enough experience to feel that we were much more powerful than she was even though we were each half her age.

I thought I might have to grab her if she bolted, but Marisol was way ahead of me and greeted the witch warmly, as if there was not a care in the world. Marisol was truly an expert at the use of her voice and body language.

"We are only here to find out what you have done with Regina, the mayor's daughter," Marisol said sweetly.

Of course, the witch denied knowing anything about it, and the more she lied, the more confident she became. Finally, with the confidence of her lies set, it appeared that she actually thought she had won out over us, and she demanded that we get out. I nearly laughed at loud when I looked over at Marisol, because I knew exactly what she was going to do next.

Marisol bent over and put both hands on the table that stood between us and the witch. This caused the front of her blouse to come down lower on her chest and expose a fake tattoo that I had helped her put on before we arrived. It was the symbol of the brujo de muerte.

The witch saw it immediately, and with lightning speed Marisol grabbed her by the wrists and pulled her upper body over the table so that they were nose to nose, and Marisol had a wicked smile on her face as she stared into her eyes. The witch screamed and began to pitifully beg for her life. She was obviously a bruja negra, but even without the fake tattoo of the witch of death she had plenty to fear from Marisol. The witch finally told us that she had sold the girl to a man in a drug cartel and that Regina was probably working in their marijuana fields in the mountains, but she had no idea where.

This was not good news at all. The drug cartels in Mexico are brutal, and even if we knew where they had her, getting her out of their hands would be next to impossible. Even the Mexican army and federal police feared the heavily armed and ruthless cartels. In this situation, being the mayor's daughter was not going to help Regina one bit. Plus, according to the witch, she had never told the man that Regina was the mayor's daughter.

Again Marisol came to the rescue, as she had already quickly formulated a plan. God, I loved to watch her work. "The mayor's daughter is mine," Marisol said in her most wicked voice that still made my skin crawl. "I have been waiting for her to bloom. She is still a virgin, but now she is ripe. I have been watching her and waiting. But then *you* took her from me. You will get her back for me so we can suck her juices or my husband will cut out your heart and stuff it down your throat."

On cue, I slowly reached into my pocket and carefully unsheathed my obsidian knife. It was so incredibly filled with power that the witch turned her head away and began to sob.

She knew immediately that I was holding no ordinary blade, and that added greatly to the legitimacy of our threats.

"But he'll never give her back," the witch said in a desperate voice. "He paid for her and was enamored with her."

"Oh, he'll give her back," Marisol replied. "You have something of this man?"

"Of course I kept some of his essence—what kind of a witch do you think I am?"

"A dead one if you don't give it to us," I said in my evilest voice while flashing her the knife.

"Okay," the witch said pitifully as Marisol released her and she went behind the curtain.

Moments later, she came back with a small jar with a brown substance inside. "This came off his muddy feet when he took his sandals off," she said in a tone that made it abundantly clear why he had taken his sandals off in her house. This was actually really good news, because the mud from his feet would have his sweat and skin in it. We had two powerful essences to be used in dreaming to find him.

"You had better not be lying," Marisol hissed. "And just so you don't botch this up, we will put the hex on this man for you. When he calls you to help him, you tell him you want the girl back as payment. He will be so desperate for a cure that he will bring the girl. When he does, you do not touch her: you call me right away. Understand?"

Before leaving the witch's house, Marisol took my knife and quickly scratched the symbol of the brujo de muerte into the table for the final effect.

Back at the car, Marisol asked if I could do my dreaming in a hotel room, and I said sure. All I needed was a candle, darkness, and quiet. "Good," she said, "it will be easier for you to find and hex this man than me. You have more in common."

"Like what?" I asked incredulously.

"Well, you both like women, for one thing."

Shrugging her comment off, we pulled out and found a hotel close to the witch's house. In our room, Marisol gave me a candle that she had in the car and told me she would wait for me in the lobby until I was finished. It was obvious that this was her plan, and I wasn't sure exactly what she wanted me to do.

"We simply need to make this guy so uncomfortable that he will call on the witch to cure him." Marisol thought for a moment, then added, "You have a snake as an ally, right? Well, how about this: using his essence, find his nagual in the underworld, and then have your snake crawl all over it until it makes him crazy. That way he won't even see you, but he sure will feel the slithery snake all over him."

I entered my dream trance as usual, flying in the underworld as a condor, but this time I was carrying the bottle with the bad man's mud. Remembering that the Lord of the Animals owed me a favor, I flew directly to him and told him what I needed to do.

"That should not be a problem," he said, taking the bottle of dirt from me. "Wait here—I'll be back."

While waiting, I summoned my snake ally and told him what was going on, and a few moments later the Lord of the Animals returned with a huge horse. "Is this the man's nagual?" I asked.

"Sure is," he replied. "Have at him—he is one of the most ornery and ill-spirited horses I have ever met. It will do him good to gain some humbleness."

My snake approached the horse, and the horse went ape. The Lord of the Animals had him tied tight to a stake, so he wasn't going anywhere. I watched as my snake began to wrap around his back leg and move toward his groin.

Confident all was going to plan, I thanked the Lord of the Animals and blew out my candle. Marisol and I called Don Vicente and gave him the update and then went for dinner. Knowing that she had lived in the city, I asked her if there was anyone she wanted to visit, but she declined by saying that we were still working and that we should probably just go back to the room and rest and wait.

It wasn't until later the next morning that we got the call. The witch was so frightened that I could clearly hear her yelling every word she said even though Marisol had her cell phone to her ear. "He's coming! He's coming! And he's very mad. He's bringing the girl, but he thinks that I am the one who hexed him! He's in agony, and I'm sure he will shoot me if I don't cure him, but I don't know how. Whatever you did to him, it worked. Please hurry!"

We arrived at the witch's house only moments after the man who had bought Regina. She was with him, and Marisol told her to go wait in our car that was parked in front of the house.

"She's not going anywhere!" the man yelled while grabbing Regina with one hand and itching himself all over with the other. He had bags under his eyes and a pained expression on his face. If he wasn't so dangerous looking, I might even have laughed.

Without a flinch, Marisol got right up in his face and looked him straight in the eye. "If you ever want to get that snake off of you, you will do exactly as I say. Understand?"

The man looked at the witch and then back at Marisol. Even though he was a drug dealer and a thug, he apparently wasn't stupid, and he grasped the situation quickly. Marisol was in charge; end of story. He let Regina go.

Marisol turned to Regina and, in keeping up our ruse, she asked, "Did this man rape you? Did he put his vile thing into you?"

"No," Regina answered, staring at the floor.

"So you're still a virgin then?"

"Yes."

"Lucky for you, mister, we can still suck her virgin juices," Marisol said in her wicked voice, turning to the man once again. "Now get the hell out of here before I send spiders crawling on you too."

"But what about the snake?" the man pleaded. "I can't stand it anymore. It's driving me crazy."

"What would you do to be rid of it?" Marisol asked, knowing full well he was at her mercy.

"Anything! Anything!"

"Listen carefully," Marisol said. "You will never use a person as a slave again. If you do, the spell of the snake will come right back onto you, and I will not be there to take it off, so more than likely it will simply torture you to death. Understand?"

The man acknowledged this and Marisol added, "Now go and release the other slaves you have working for you. Once you have done that, the spell will be released."

I never saw anyone get in their car faster. And as he screeched away, Marisol dealt harshly with the witch by going into her back room and taking many valuable items from her as payment for stealing her virgin and wasting her time.

We took Regina home. On the way, we told her that we were not evil witches, but I'm not sure to what extent she actually believed us. Mayor Rodriguez was so impressed with our work that he hired Marisol to perform healings on each member of his family, and he is now a believer in witchcraft and retains Marisol as a consultant and an advisor.

Two days after we brought Regina home, Marisol felt sure that the bad man had freed all the slaves, so I lifted my snake from his horse. The Lord of the Animals simply smirked at me as the look on the horse's face told us both he would never make trouble again...

———

the "love" spell

on Vicente came to my room and told me there was a young woman waiting to see me in his office. When I looked at him quizzically, he simply commented that she had come to him for a healing but that he wanted me to handle it.

Her name was Lilly, and she was from the United States, but her husband was an executive for a company with a big plant in Veracruz City, and they had been living in Mexico on and off for over a year. I could tell she was slightly embarrassed talking to me, so I assured her that nothing she said would cause me to judge her and that she could speak freely with me. By the way she was fidgeting, I had the distinct feeling that she was a cheating wife, and I was right. And, as you will hear, the circumstances turned out to be anything but normal.

"My husband's best friend here, Rob, also is from the US, and they work at the plant together," she began. "I'm not super close with his wife, but we're friends, and they come over with their family for cookouts and stuff, and we go over to their house sometimes too. Anyway, one time about two months ago, we were over at their house having some drinks, and one of Rob's friends, Xavier, was there—and I took one look at him, and my heart melted.

"Now, don't get me wrong: I would never cheat on my husband just because I found Xavier to be the most attractive man I'd ever met. I'm not like that. But he gave me his card because he's a contractor and we had some work we wanted to have done at our house. Long story short, he came over and met with my husband and me, and we hired him to remodel our kitchen and build a small deck. Since my husband works long hours, I admit it was nice to have him and his workers around. Sometimes I get bored when my husband is gone for twelve hours a day and then comes home tired. But even though Xavier and I became very friendly, nothing ever happened between us that was inappropriate.

"Until one day—it was a Saturday, and Xavier was not coming over but my husband had to work, so I went shopping. Well, window shopping—I don't even think I bought anything. But the whole day I couldn't stop thinking about Xavier. Everywhere I went and anyone I talked to somehow reminded me of him. I'd never felt anything like it before. I missed him so badly it was making me crazy. When I got home that night and took a bath, I felt a little better, but I also felt extremely guilty about having all those thoughts, and it was hard for me to even face my husband. The next day, Sunday, we took a trip up the coast, and even being with my husband, I couldn't stop thinking of Xavier.

"On Monday morning I had appointments, and I couldn't wait to get home and see Xavier. But he hadn't shown up for work, which was not like him at all. I tried calling him but he didn't answer. I needed to see him so bad that I went looking for him. I found him at home...and I did something inexcusable."

Lilly stared at the floor the whole time she was talking and didn't even look at me once.

"Anything else?" I inquired.

"I have been with him almost every day since then. It's crazy. I love my husband. He's kind and funny, and he treats me like a princess. I would never leave him. But Xavier has this hold on me. We never do anything at my house, but every time I leave to go somewhere, I end up with him at his house or somewhere else. Lately I've been intentionally staying home so I don't have the urge to see him. It's like whenever I leave my house I'm drawn to him like a magnet. It's like he has a spell on me or something."

With the word *spell* finally out on the table, Lilly looked up at me with tears in her eyes.

"Can you help me?" she pleaded.

"Well, that depends," I answered. "Did Don Vicente tell you I would need a personal item of yours? Something that is very close to you?"

"Yes, he suggested I give you my cross necklace," she said as she removed it from her neck. "I hardly ever take it off."

"That's perfect," I replied. "Come back this same time tomorrow, and we'll talk some more." I quickly cut a paper figure of a protector spirit for her and gave it to her as she was leaving.

I watched as she put it in her purse, and that made me feel like I had at least done something for her.

That evening in my dream trance I clutched Lilly's necklace and learned a lot about her. She was honest and caring and loyal—not the kind of person that would be sneaking around on her husband without a darn good reason. But I neither saw nor felt anything that would explain her actions. The next morning I called her and asked if she could bring me something of Xavier's.

When she arrived, I admitted to her that I didn't have any answers yet. While handing me a hammer that she had taken from the deck Xavier was building, she admitted to me that she stopped and saw Xavier on the way home after leaving me last evening.

I could hardly believe it. I had thought for sure that summoning a protector spirit for her would have been enough to keep her away from him for at least one day! It was then that I realized for sure that someone had witched her.

In my dream trance with Xavier's hammer, I understood for certain that he was a brujo pequeno and that Lilly wasn't the only woman he had under his spell. But I still couldn't see how he was doing it. Don Vicente was away, so I called Marisol. She suggested that I dream with Lilly's necklace again, because Xavier didn't even need to be around her for her to want him.

In trance with her necklace again, I went through almost a full day with Lilly and found nothing unusual. I called Marisol again, and she came over.

"Okay, so tell me about the dream," she said.

"Typical stuff," I replied. "She did housework, laundry, watched some TV, talked to her husband and a few other people on the phone, and then the next thing you know she grabs her purse on the way to the video store and ends up at Xavier's place. I have no idea why."

"Wait—back up," Marisol said as if on to something. "You made a point to say she grabbed her purse. Why?"

"I don't know. I was just telling you what she did."

"But didn't you also tell me that when Lilly is at home she doesn't feel the urge for Xavier as strong, but when she leaves the house, for some reason that's when she goes to Xavier's?"

"Yeah."

"Don't you see? It's the purse! Whenever she's carrying the purse, she gets pulled to him."

I immediately called Lilly and told her to come over right away and to make sure to bring her purse. When she arrived, Marisol asked if she could see the purse; coming from a woman, I think it made Lilly more comfortable. The purse was not overly large, but it wasn't small either, and it seemed to be fairly full of stuff.

Marisol slid her hand inside and expertly felt around the inside of the liner until she found what she was looking for. "Aha!" she said triumphantly. "Lilly, would you mind if I dumped your purse on the table? There's something here you should see."

"Go right ahead."

"James, go and get me a razor knife from the desk," Marisol instructed me as she dumped out the contents of the purse.

With the purse empty, Marisol carefully cut a small opening in the liner of the purse and pulled out a small item wrapped in plastic about two inches long that had been sewn into the lining. Placing it on the table, she unwrapped it as Lilly and I stared in awe. It was a dried hummingbird.

"Hummingbirds are one of the most powerful items for a little witch like this Xavier fellow," Marisol said in a voice that let me know she wasn't too impressed. "They can carry quite a potent love spell. Well, not really *love*, mind you, but…"

"We get the point, Marisol," I said, cutting her off.

"Oh, sorry," she said, blushing. "I'll just go and get the antidote."

Marisol came back a few minutes later from her father's workroom with a small silver locket and handed it to Lilly. "This locket is filled with a powder from a praying mantis. Most people don't know this, but a praying mantis is so fast and agile it can even catch a hummingbird and eat it. The mantis powder is the strongest cure for the hummingbird spell that Xavier placed on you. Put that locket on your necklace, and now that the hummingbird is gone from your purse, you should be free from his spell. In fact, after he gets close to you the first time, he will probably avoid you altogether after that. I'm sure he will feel the power of the mantis that you carry, and he will be afraid to even get close to you."

The moment Lilly added the locket to her necklace, a fresh breeze blew through the room, and for the first time since we met, Lilly smiled radiantly.

———

good witch, bad witch

Walking through the city one day, I noticed that there was a large line of people waiting outside the home of one of the resident witches. This was certainly not common. Successful healers and witches may sometimes see multiple clients in one day, but for one of us to actually have so much business that a line forms was completely out of the ordinary, and I made a mental note to speak to Don Vicente about it.

When I got home to his place later, Marisol was there, and Don Vicente and she were conversing on the back patio, so I joined them. Not surprisingly, they were already talking about the bang-up business that the healer/witch Tania was suddenly doing. Don Vicente quickly caught me up on the conversation. It turned out that a number of other healers/witches had come to him that morning to report and complain about Tania. Even though healers and witches have their own personal practices, there is also an underlying camaraderie between most of them, and when problematic situations arise they will often band together for the greater good, like in Rafael's case.

Since Don Vicente was considered a leader in the witch community and known to be very fair, the other witches had come to him for help, because their businesses had dropped to barely nothing in the previous weeks. For some reason, everyone was now going to Tania for healings, and the other witches obviously smelled foul play.

Don Vicente was in a very good mood that day and was making jokes the whole time he was telling us about the situation. He chuckled extra hard as he showed me the stack of cash the other witches had brought him to clear up this problem. He gave the money to Marisol and told us to rent a room across the street from Tania's house and to watch that night after she closed her office to see who came by. He had the feeling that Tania was playing the good witch–bad witch scam.

This is a typical ploy in many cultures that employ folk healers and witches. The ruse is simple: one witch hexes or poisons people, and the other witch cures them; then they split the profit. It's a great way for a tandem of witches to make money, but in the witch fraternity it is taboo and levies a strict punishment if the witches are caught.

Luckily for us, Tania had a single dwelling with a gate to the walkway of her house, so it would be easy for us to see who came and went. But just to be sure we had our bases covered, Marisol suggested that I cover the back entrance to the house as well. So, around midnight, I stationed myself in the alley while Marisol watched the front.

Around 2 AM Tania had a visitor come to the back door, and luckily she didn't see me. It was one of the female gypsy Hungaros, easily identified by her unique style of colorful dress. When I first found out about the Hungaros a few months before, I was immediately fascinated, as both of my parents were born in Hungary, although they were not gypsies. These Hungaros were descended from Hungarian roots, but they were definitely gypsies and were known for soliciting tourists on the malecon (the popular walkway that runs along the lake) for palm and tarot card readings, selling trinkets and amulets, and sometimes swindling people with parlor tricks. I had to laugh to myself that the "bad" witch in this duo was probably the Hungaro gypsy. A few minutes later, she left Tania's. I took close note of her dress, because they usually owned only one, and headed back to tell Marisol.

"I wish you would have been there instead of me," I said to Marisol. "You could have gotten a hair or something else from her without startling her. All I have is the color and design of her dress."

"No worries, James," Don Vicente said as Marisol and I were eating breakfast with him the next morning. "We have enough to proceed with this situation. What we need to know now is exactly how the gypsy is witching people."

Marisol suggested that she go in disguise and look around the market and the malecon the gypsies frequented. She was sure she could find the gypsy by my description of her dress, and she was right. It took her only a few hours to locate her, and by dinnertime we were all chatting once again.

"James, why don't you go to Tania's after dinner? Since she prefers to work in the evening, there will probably be a line of people there again. Go and talk with them, and find out what they are doing there. They are more likely to give you information than me or Marisol," Don Vicente said.

I agreed and quickly found out that most of the people in line were complaining of a specific rash. Some of the people said that they had gone to other healers but that Tania was the only one with a cure, thus the line of people waiting to see her. When I asked how they had gotten the rash, no one could come up with a definitive answer. But one thing was for sure: all the people in line were locals, and most of them worked on the malecon.

The next day Marisol found the answer while spying on the gypsy. Turns out she had acquired some spools of rope and was selling it very cheap. Rope is pretty much used for everything in Mexico, and in this case it was an extremely popular item because all of the tarps that were hung on the wooden booths of the malecon vendors were secured with rope. I was sent to buy some from the gypsy and bring it back to Don Vicente. After that was complete, Don Vicente asked Don Julio to go and buy some. A visit from a brujo de muerte such as Don Julio is enough to scare anyone, and chances were that the gypsy was not a witch but merely hired by Tania to sell the witched rope. The plan worked perfectly. As soon as the gypsy saw Don Julio standing in front of her, she knew the jig was up, and she bolted. One problem solved.

"How do *you* feel?" Don Vicente asked me slyly. I knew from the tone of his voice and the comical look on his face that he was up to something, and then it hit me. How could I have been so naïve? He sent me to buy the rope so that I would get the darn rash. Not only that, but now I was extremely worried because I had just been to the restroom and had touched myself in places I sure as hell did not want a rash.

With a flicker of comprehension in his eyes as to what I was thinking, I jokingly told Don Vicente that he was an evil old man and that he shouldn't be tricking his apprentice with rashes, especially in that region of the body.

He just laughed and said that it was just one of the many lessons I still needed to learn. "You could have worn gloves," he added with a laugh.

"Or had her put it in a bag for you," Marisol added.

"Or washed your hands before touching your wiener," Don Julio said as all three of them roared with laughter.

"The good thing," Don Vicente said as they calmed down, "is that soon you will have the rash and can visit with Tania without raising suspicion." Of course this had been my teacher's plan from the beginning.

"But don't you think the gypsy will tell her about Don Julio?" I asked.

"Probably, but if Tania is willing to flaunt this scam of hers in front of everyone, I bet she's greedy enough to see the last patients from the rash and take their money."

"So what do you want me to do?" I asked.

"Well, Tania obviously witched the rope with something— more than likely a type of powder that would get on people's hands and then spread. You'll probably have the rash by morning, so you'll want to go over to Tania's and get her cure, which

I guess will be some kind of simple salve, but she'll probably dress it up and turn it into a whole healing session to get more money. She may even insist that you come back for a second session."

The next morning I did indeed have the rash on various places on my body. I went to see Tania and was surprised to find that she was very young, maybe twenty years old at the most. But even though she hid it well, I could tell that she was secretly distraught. There was something in her life that was tearing her apart.

As Don Vicente had predicted, she gave me a special salve for the rash, and she did a hands-on healing ceremony for me and told me to come back in two days for a follow-up session. Because she was only a bruja pequena, she didn't feel or see who I truly was. In a way, I simply felt sorry for her, even though she was swindling people and causing a ruckus in the witch community. Before I left, I invented the ruse that Americans always hugged their doctors (most Mexican people I know are not prone to hugging strangers), and so I was able to easily obtain Tania's hair to dream with.

But in my dream trance I didn't see Tania at all. I saw a little girl about two years old lying in a bed, with her tonalli (soul) barely attached to her body. She was dying, and without help she wouldn't last much longer. I told Don Vicente what I saw, and he suggested I call Don Julio, since he was also a medical doctor.

I explained to Don Julio what I saw. "Yes, well, Tania has a two-year-old daughter," he said. "I delivered her. Wasn't she there when you went for the healing?"

"If she was, I didn't see her," I replied.

"From what you have told me, I would guess her daughter is very sick and maybe is in a hospital. Tania probably cooked up the good witch–bad witch scheme to raise money for the bills she is acquiring. I will meet you at Tania's at 10 AM tomorrow, and we will find out what is going on. Ask Vicente, Marisol, and Florinda to come with you."

The next day we went to Tania's, and I was surprised to see that Don Julio had brought over a dozen other witch-healers with him. When Tania saw all of us, she began to weep and told us the whole story. Her daughter was in a special children's hospital in Mexico City, and she readily admitted to hexing the rope and making money on the cure in order to pay for her daughter's hospital bills.

"Why didn't you ask us for help?" Don Julio inquired.

"I guess I was too proud and didn't know if anyone would help me," she replied.

Marisol gave her the rest of the money that the witches had given to Don Vicente to deal with her, and all the other witches gave her more money as well. It was agreed that Tania should bring her daughter back to Catemaco, and over the course of many weeks Don Julio cured her with both traditional medicine and dreaming practices to restore her soul. During that time Tania and I became friends, and Florinda became her new teacher. What began as a bad situation ended up being a blessing for both Tania and her daughter.

bloodsucker

One of the most disturbing cases I've ever worked on involved the *tlahuelpuchi*, a class of brujo de muerte that specializes in sucking the blood of infants less than one year of age, killing them. It was Don Julio who received the original call for help on the case, and after visiting the rural town where it was happening, he brought Don Vicente, Florinda, Marisol, and myself in to help. Our first meeting about this case was at Don Julio's home.

"I'm sad to say that I have confirmed the existence of at least one tlahuelpuchi in Tlaxcala (a small state to the southwest of the Tuxtlas)," Don Julio began. "Even though our teachers had eradicated them in that area back in the '60s, I knew it was inevitable that this would happen again sooner or later."

Don Vicente and Florinda sat rigid in their chairs, and although I wouldn't say that they were scared, this was the most concerned I had ever seen them. Looking at me and reading my mind, Marisol said, "Don Julio, James and I have never heard of the tlahuelpuchi. What can you tell us?"

"The tlahuelpuchi is always a woman. She is born with the affliction of needing to suck on a live baby's blood once every month after she has her first menstruation. The existence of the tlahuelpuchi has been documented for thousands of years. In modern times, there have been anthropologists such as Hugo Nutini who have studied the phenomenon. Nutini and others examined the cases of hundreds of suspected deaths at the hands of the tlahuelpuchi in the 1960s, but of the forty-seven infant corpses he examined, more than two-thirds of them were found not to be the work of a tlahuelpuchi. The most common cause of death was determined to be suffocation. Women in those rural villages tend to breastfeed their babies to sleep at night, and sometimes they fall asleep too and accidentally roll onto the baby in the night so that the baby can't breath. Cases also involved choking to death and infanticide.

"You see, from time immemorial, people, especially mothers who loved their babies, had to come up with some kind of an explanation for when an infant died. This is probably how the legend of the tlahuelpuchi began. But that wasn't the only reason. To blame a tlahuelpuchi for an infant's death was common practice all the way to modern times, because the tlahuelpuchi actually do exist. Unlike the more common brujo de muerte who kills for power or even for hire and then sucks the juices of the corpse, the tlahuelpuchi needs live human blood, and the pure blood of an infant is always their first choice and is usually the easiest to get. I have studied this phenomenon for over forty years and have been called on cases many times in the past. This is the first time I have seen actual evidence of a tlahuelpuchi since when I was a teenager."

"But how do they do it? How can someone get away with sucking the blood of a baby and not get caught?" I asked.

"Well, first of all," Don Vicente told us, "the tlahuelpuchi is an ordinary person in their everyday life. They almost always have a job, a husband, and may even go to church. In fact, even though they are obviously feared for what they do—and killed if found out—in most communities that believe in the tlahuelpuchi, the people don't even blame the woman for what she is. It is simply a part of their culture.

"Also, the tlahuelpuchi is a powerful witch and works with the airs of spirits in a similar way to how we do. When she enters a house through a window or door, she conjures a wind that places a deep sleeping spell on everyone in the house. It is also documented that they can appear as animals and go unnoticed as they search for a victim. The tlahuelpuchi is a formidable opponent."

"And that's why I've gathered the best witches in the Tuxtlas to help," said Don Julio. "If you are willing, we will meet here at dawn tomorrow and drive to the village of Huatulco and begin our witch hunt."

The next morning we met at Don Julio's and took his large SUV on the long drive to Huatulco. We each had one small bag with similar contents. Mine included my box of paper-cut spirits, takwatzi, candles, and a few extra clothes. The mood in the truck was all business, unlike the jovial atmosphere that usually surrounded my witch friends.

When we arrived at the rural village of Huatulco, we went straight to the vacant house that Mr. Ortiz, the head witch of the area, had acquired for us to use, and he was there waiting for us. Unfortunately, the tlahuelpuchi had struck again the night before.

"This is very unusual for a tlahuelpuchi," Ortiz said. "Normally a tlahuelpuchi will kill only once a month. This tlahuelpuchi is now acting more like a serial killer and must be stopped right away. I gathered the community together this morning, and even though everyone has already heard the news, I suggested that all families with babies have at least one family member stay up all night guarding the baby. But since that might not be enough to keep the tlahuelpuchi away, I also instructed them to place a small mirror on the baby's chest or in the crib."

"Very good," replied Don Julio as he turned to Marisol and me. "A mirror is one of the most effective defenses against the tlahuelpuchi. Even if she is able to put a spell on the people in the house, if the baby has a mirror it will dissuade the witch, and she will have to search for another victim. I have no doubt that she has already heard that we are here, so she will be extra careful. But her killing has escalated beyond her basic need for blood, so our presence will not likely stop her from trying to kill again."

Don Julio asked Ortiz to take us to the house of the latest victim, and much to my chagrin we began walking to the house a few minutes later. When we arrived, Florinda and Marisol went to speak with the mother and the other women of the household while the rest of us spoke with the men of the family.

According to Don Julio, it was a classic case of a tlahuel-puchi killing. There was a window found standing open, the whole family had overslept and needed to be awakened in the morning by a neighbor, and upon examination of the baby, a human bite mark was found on the back of the baby's neck. The baby also showed signs of asphyxiation such as petechial hemorrhages in the eyes. I had never seen a dead infant before, and it turned my stomach. If it wasn't for being surrounded by my teachers and the fact that I was there to help, I doubt very seriously that I could have handled the situation. For sure, I would never have taken this case alone, and now I fully understood why Don Julio had asked us for help. It probably had more to do with being in the company of his good friends than him actually needing help in catching the witch. There was something so awfully wrong about murdering babies that even Don Julio was not immune to the psychological effects.

That evening, we ate dinner at a restaurant with Ortiz and a dozen other men and devised our plan. At dusk, Ortiz and his men would stand guard at intersections of the town's streets and watch for suspicious activity. Don Julio reminded the men that the tlahuelpuchi could appear as an animal, most likely a dog, while she was searching for a victim. Since Huatulco was a typical Mexican village with lots of dogs running around, especially at night, this made a perfect cover for the witch.

It was decided that we witches from Tuxtlas would go to seek help from Matlalcuéyetl, so a few hours later I found myself hiking with my teachers to the base of the inactive volcano just outside the village. The peak of the Matlalcuéyetl volcano is the sixth highest in Mexico and is known by the locals as the goddess of song and of rain. We made a small fire and sat in a circle around it, with the top of the volcano looming behind us.

Taking our cue from Florinda, the expert dreamer of our group, we each took out paper and scissors from our spirit boxes and then went deep into a dream-trance state. I don't know what any of my companions saw, but the first vision I had was of a very small silver dog running down the street in the moonlight. It appeared to be a purebred chihuahua and not one of the mixed-breed dogs so common to the streets of Mexico and often referred to as dingos. The dog was going from house to house as if it was lost and searching for its home. My next vision was entirely different. In this vision, I was looking down on a house as if I were hovering above it. I could detect five people inside the house, but the image was very similar to what I'd seen of infrared videos that show the heat patterns of people. Near the back of the house was a large heat source, and right next to it a tiny one: mother and baby.

My third vision was of men carrying a naked young woman out of a deep ravine on a gurney. She was obviously dead, and her body was mangled and bloody as if she had fallen from a cliff and bounced off the walls several times before hitting the bottom. When the men brought her out of the ravine, I looked into her staring eyes, and in that moment mine popped open.

All of us came out of our dream trance at nearly the same moment, but already Florinda was standing and calling out to the immense spirit of Matlalcuéyetl to come to our aid. My impression was that Florinda wanted to use the powerful spirit against the witch because it would be one that the witch was already familiar with since she lived so close to it.

Feeling the spirit wind of Matlalcuéyetl, we all rapidly cut the figure in paper and held it in our hands as we hiked back to the village with our trance-dream visions fresh in our minds. We reached the edge of town, and Ortiz was waiting for us and handed each of us a small square mirror. I wrapped my paper figure around the mirror so I could carry both in the same hand.

Don Julio motioned for us to spread out, and we each took a different street and walked through the town. A little while later we all ended up at the same small house on the opposite end of town. Ortiz showed up a few minutes later and told us that a young widow lived in the house. Her husband had been killed in a car accident just two weeks ago, and the widow was still in mourning.

"Isn't that about the time the baby killings first started?" Don Julio asked.

"Well, yeah, I guess it was," he replied. "I hadn't even thought of that."

"Tlahuelpuchi will always have a husband or brother or sister who knows about them and who will help them even though they know what the witch does. Sometimes it's out of fear or even love that they do it. If this woman is the witch and her husband was her helper and he died suddenly, that could be what triggered her killing spree. A tlahuelpuchi needs a loyal helper to deal with the normal world and keep up her disguise. And I saw a dead man in a car in my dream trance," Don Julio said.

"And I saw a young woman dressed in black at a funeral," Marisol added.

"Well, we can't just go accusing her of being the tlahuelpuchi without solid proof," Ortiz chimed in.

"Agreed," said Don Vicente.

So once again we split up and walked through the town. But after a couple hours, Don Vicente gathered us together at the house and said that we needed to be more proactive and that he had a plan.

"More than likely the witch doesn't know that we are using this particular house since we just arrived today. And if the witch is the widow, which I'll bet she is, then she will have a hard time keeping up with the town gossip without her husband, so there's a chance she doesn't know that we're here. So let's set a little trap."

"I'll do it!" Marisol said enthusiastically, without even hearing her father's plan.

Don Vicente just chuckled and smiled at his daughter. "You always were one step ahead of me. Okay, here's the plan," Don Vicente said to the rest of us. "Marisol will stay here in the house. James, you and Florinda hide and watch the front of the house, and Don Julio and I will watch the back. When we're ready, Marisol will make the sounds of a baby crying. I know it sounds way too simple and easy, but I'm willing to bet that the witch will not be able to resist checking it out. It's so quiet in this town right now that a crying baby is sure to lure her in, especially with her recent lust for blood."

Marisol cried on and off for about an hour when I noticed movement in the shadows around the corner of the house. A small dog emerged, but it saw one of Ortiz's men and made a wide detour around him.

"I saw that dog in my dream trance," I whispered to Florinda.

"Yeah, me too," she said to me with a grin.

The little silver chihuahua made it to the street in front of the house and then quickly went to one of the side windows of the house that Florinda and I could clearly see. It then began jumping up and down to get a glimpse in the window that was many feet above its head. If the situation weren't so deadly serious, it would have been comical.

Still crying like a baby, Marisol must have spotted the jumping chihuahua, because in a flash she appeared in the window holding her mirror in one hand and the cut figure of Matlalcuéyetl in the other.

The dog yelped and darted away, but it had no idea who it was dealing with. Florinda, Don Julio, and Don Vicente were such masters of the dream body that they all could easily make themselves appear in two places at once when the need arose. Florinda immediately flew with her dream body and appeared right in the dog's path. It turned to run, but right behind it stood Don Julio. It took off between them and headed toward the woods on the edge of town. I ran after it, with Marisol close behind me.

We chased it for about half a mile until the little dog began to run out of gas. One of the downfalls to the tlahuelpuchi animal form is that it cannot make the animal any stronger or faster than it naturally is. But the little dog kept running until it came to the edge of a deep ravine. Florinda, Don Vicente, and Don Julio stepped out from the trees and cornered the dog. Marisol and I stopped about twenty yards away and watched as the little dog transformed into a naked young woman—the same woman I had seen in my dream trance.

Immediately I knew what was going to happen. But Florinda began to speak to the woman, and even though I couldn't make out what she was saying, I knew she was trying to get her to confess for what she had done and to come with them peacefully.

The young woman simply stood calmly on the edge of the ravine, said a few words to them, and then actually bowed to them in respect. In that moment, I thought she might just simply surrender to them, but in the next instant she quickly turned and silently jumped headfirst into the deep ravine and to her obvious death.

Ortiz begged us to stay, but we did not want to be part of the spectacle that would happen in the morning when the witch's death was discovered. We all wanted to just go home and put Huatulco behind us. Needless to say, the baby deaths in Huatulco ended that night.

———

aztec warrior

I know how strange this may sound," Shiori said, "but our son is not our son anymore."

"We don't know what to do. We've been to doctors and therapists, shamans and folk healers, and he still is not himself. Something is terribly wrong with him," Demian, Shiori's husband, added.

"Let's start at the beginning," I suggested.

Shiori, Demian, and I sat outside on the covered patio at Don Vicente's as they told me about the problems they were having with their nineteen-year-old son, Victor.

"At first, it seemed innocent enough," Shiori began. "They were studying Aztec-Mexica history in his history class at school, and Victor really got into it. He received As on all his reports and projects and was completely enthralled by the ancient Aztec culture. Since Vic isn't normally an A student and gets easily distracted, his focus on the Aztecs seemed very positive. But after the class moved on to study another culture, Vic didn't want to, and that's when we began to get concerned.

"Then, while researching universities he wanted to attend after high school, he learned about *Movimiento Estudiantil Chicano de Aztlán* (MEChA), the Chicano Student Movement of Aztlán that has over 400 chapters in the United States. Most of them are on university campuses. He became so obsessed with wanting to go to school in the United States that he spent all of his time studying, improving his grades, and preparing for the entry exams. He succeeded in getting a scholarship to UCLA, which has one of the largest MEChA chapters in the country. Even though MEChA does some very good things to support Mexican Americans, Victor fell into the offshoot radical groups that call themselves La Raza (The Race), and they are racist toward everyone that doesn't have bloodlines to the indigenous peoples of Mexico.

"Basically their view is that Mexicans living in the southwest United States should not be seen as immigrants, or illegals, because that land is part of their birthright. They claim all lands given up by Mexico in the Mexican-American war to be Aztlán, the ancient home of the Aztecs. According to them, Aztlán includes all land of the Treaty of Guadalupe, which ended the war in 1848 and encompasses Texas, New Mexico, Arizona, California, Utah, Nevada, and parts of Colorado and Wyoming."

"Living in Arizona, I am well aware of the ongoing border and immigration problems," I replied. "It's a hot topic for sure, but there are literally millions of people involved with this. I get the feeling there is more to Victor's story than political activism."

"Yes, that was just the beginning," Shiori said. "After his first year at UCLA, he came home to Mexico City, but he was not the same. He came back home with a hatred for the United States government and for Americans not of Latino descent. Victor and his gang began robbing and stealing from American tourists. I found wallets and jewelry hidden in his room. And I also know from speaking with other parents and the police that they often travel to Cancún and Acapulco to seduce American girls or even rape them before robbing them. This is not our son. He was raised to be polite and respectful and has never been in trouble before.

"But the worst part is for the last few months he has changed even more. He talks differently. His voice and his speech patterns are completely different. And he dresses like some kind of Aztec warrior. It's as if there is someone else living in Victor's body."

"Has he been to any Aztec archeological sites?" I asked, even though I guessed the answer was obvious.

"Oh, yes," Shiori replied. "When still in high school he spent lots of time at the Templo Mayor (an ancient sacred site in the heart of Mexico City), and he and his friends made many trips to Teotihuacan, Tula, and Xochicalco, and I believe they still visit these and other sites all the time, sometimes spending many days there. The last we knew, Victor was living in Xochimilco." (Xochimilco is in the south of Mexico City and known for its system of canals and waterways similar to the ancient Aztec capital of Tenochtitlan.)

Listening to Shiori and Demian, my gut feeling was that a spirit had attached itself to Victor while he was visiting one of the ancient Aztec sacred sites. He was the perfect candidate for a spirit possession by those that he venerated. But I also now knew that reaching Victor, or even talking to him at all, would be extremely difficult. According to Victor's parents, he now spoke almost exclusively in Nahuatl, the language of the Aztecs. Luckily for me, my sister-witch Marisol was fluent in Nahuatl, and I immediately called and asked for her help.

With Marisol's help and by speaking to lots of people around the city, we were able to locate Victor and his crew. He was at the Zócalo, the giant main square in the heart of the historic center of Mexico City, where he was participating in a public Aztec dance and ceremony. The dance and ceremony were beautiful, and hundreds of people joined in. It made me wonder how this peaceful dance and ceremony could involve such radicals and criminals as Victor and his friends.

Marisol and I decided it would be better to approach Victor without bringing up his parents or anything else that might turn him against us until we gained his trust, or at least tried to. Victor was one of the lead drummers in the ceremony, and he was packing up his things at the conclusion when Marisol addressed him in Nahuatl.

"Greetings, my brother," Marisol said. "That was a beautiful ceremony. My friend and I are visiting from Veracruz, and we were hoping for the chance to meet people who are keeping the ancient traditions alive."

Victor stood up straight and looked down at Marisol with piercing brown eyes. He was tall, handsome, and extremely muscular. His jet-black hair was much longer than the photos his parents had provided of him, and in his ceremonial costume Victor certainly looked the part of an Aztec warrior or priest. I immediately agreed with his parents that his powerful demeanor was not that of a typical nineteen-year-old college student.

"Greetings," replied Victor. "It is music to my ears to hear our ancient language spoken so eloquently by such a gorgeous woman. La Raza (the Race) runs strongly in you. But why do you travel with this gringo?" he said, turning to look me unkindly in the eye.

"He is no ordinary gringo," Marisol said. "He is a powerful tetlachihuic trained in the ancient arts."

"Ha, ha, ha, you make me laugh, woman," Victor said, "but laughter comes too seldom in these times of trouble. Come on and tell me some more of your jokes. A gringo tetlachihuic, an Aztec witch-healer—now that's a good one."

Hearing Victor's voice, I had no doubt that we were dealing with a case of spirit possession and that the spirit inhabiting Victor would ruthlessly defend or even gladly die for the cause he believed in. Until I proved myself to him, I would be in mortal danger around this man and his companions. So without outwardly showing it, I prepared myself internally and consciously raised my level of awareness to his every move while I also secretly unsheathed my obsidian knife.

As I predicted, Victor stepped toward me and insulted me quite proficiently in Mexico City Spanish slang. Hearing this, a few of his companions drew near and surrounded me. They moved Marisol away, and she stole a knowing glance at me as I surveyed the situation. She knew I had to get out of this myself and prove to Victor what she had told him about me. I actually wasn't too worried, because as I looked into the eyes of Victor and his companions, I could see that even though they may be racists, thieves, and even rapists, they also were in deep connection to the ancient sacred sites, and because of this they would be able to see my spirit allies if I called them to me.

But I didn't even need to make the call. In times of trouble my allies naturally come. As Victor insulted me, I actually laughed because Itzamna was standing next to him and mimicking him in the most comical fashion. And my wolves sat calmly behind him, staring intently. I could see Victor's wrath build at my laughter, but as he looked to his companions, they began to back away from me. They obviously saw Itzamna and my wolves.

Victor hadn't yet seen my allies, but even if he did he probably would have came at me anyway. He quickly reached out to grab my neck, but I was ready for him and, taking him off-guard, I easily tripped him backwards to the ground, and in one swift motion I was on top of him, with my blade at his throat. Instantly my wolves converged, growling, and I saw recognition in Victor's eyes as he looked over at both my wolves and felt the power of my ancient knife.

"Well met, tetlachihuic," Victor said as I let him up and he looked at Itzamna with wonder. "These are interesting times, for sure, when a gringo can spring from nowhere wielding a blade of our ancestors and be accompanied by such powerful and interesting spirits."

Itzamna merely bowed, and with a smirk he and my wolves walked into the crowd and disappeared.

Smiling radiantly as if enjoying herself immensely, Marisol came over to us. "Now that that's settled, how about we get to know each other better," Marisol said directly to Victor. With a glint in his eye, as he made it quite obvious he was looking Marisol up and down, Victor replied, "Tonight we have much to do, and no offense, but women are not allowed."

I caught the irritation in Marisol's eyes because I knew her so well, but she casually brushed off the insult to her ego and replied in her happy-go-lucky manner, "Okay, but maybe we shall meet again. I'm Marisol, and this is James," she said, extending her hand.

Victor took her hand and then gently raised it to his lips and kissed it as he got on one knee and then rose again. "Well met, Marisol," he said knowingly. "Am I not wrong in my intuition that you are a tetlachihuic as well?"

Marisol didn't answer the question directly, but everything about her provided the answer without words, and for a few moments, as Marisol looked up and into Victor's face, it seemed that she had entranced him and that time had stopped.

Marisol released her gaze, and Victor said, "In any case, it seems we shall meet again, Marisol. My name is Huitzilo-pochtli. The tetlachihuic Ulu Temay may join us tonight if he wishes, and we will see you in the morning."

Hiding our shock that Victor referred to himself as Huitzilo-pochtli, one of the most powerful Aztec deities, and that he called me by my Wirrarika name, which he couldn't possibly have known, Marisol looked over at me and nonchalantly said,

"Sure, if Ulu Temay will join you, I will go and visit with some friends. Call me in the morning."

Not giving me a chance to respond, she quickly turned and walked away, leaving me with Victor, aka Huitzilopochtli, and his crew. "Damn witches," I thought to myself for the hundredth time as I couldn't help silently laughing at Marisol's skill and decisiveness. We both had many friends in Mexico City, so I knew she would be just fine as we watched her leave. In that moment, the only person I was worried about was myself.

A short drive later, we arrived at a home in a very upscale neighborhood. Upon entering, it looked like this was the headquarters for Victor and his small army. There were banners and posters of many La Raza–type organizations covering the walls, but more importantly and much to my chagrin there were also weapons of every kind leaning against the walls and stored in lockers. Hanging on the wall above a large table in the dining room was a map of the United States with dozens of cities marked in various colors of marker.

"This is our network," Victor said as he pointed to the map. "All of these states here will be ours again soon," he added while pointing to the states to the west side of a thick line drawn on the map. The states included Texas, New Mexico, Arizona, California, Utah, Nevada, Colorado, and Wyoming, just as his mother had told us. "All this land belongs to us, the ancient home of our ancestors; it's only a matter of time until we take it back."

Just then Victor's cell phone rang, and he walked into another large room. Following behind him, I was stunned to see several young men working at tables with sewing machines, and in the far corner was another man with a triple-beam scale, weighing and bagging what appeared to be a large amount of cocaine. A chill ran down my spine, and I suddenly felt that I had gotten involved with something completely over my head. The men at the sewing machines were apparently sewing the bags of cocaine inside the backpacks to conceal them.

Finished with his call, Victor turned to me. "So what do you think, tetlachihuic?"

"I don't understand," I replied. "Why the need for illegal drugs? Huitzilopochtli is the name of a warrior god. If you are truly a warrior, why do you need all this?"

"Because this is the only way we can fight right now. We cannot wage war on the United States with weapons. But we can infect them by preying on their righteous weaknesses. All those white fools at the university give us their parents' money to snort my weapon up their noses. They are actually paying us for our war against them."

Even though what Victor was doing was incredibly wrong, I could see the logic behind his dementia. Just as with the Mexican-American war that took the lands Victor claimed as Aztlán, there was no way Mexico or La Raza could win militarily over the United States.

"This 'war on drugs' is the new war—a war that we are actually winning!" Victor said loudly for all to hear. "And you know why? Because Americans can't stop putting this stuff up their noses and in their arms. They are weak and fat and lazy. If Americans would stop using drugs, what would happen? We would all be out of business, that's what. No more drug cartels, no more dirty politicians, no more smuggling and fighting.

Don't you see? The Americans feed all this by their consumption. We are not to blame for their bad habit, we are merely exploiting them because we can. And that will be their downfall.

"Come, Ulu Temay," Victor said as he led me back to the dining room. "Our couriers will be here soon to take our latest weapons across the border. With our student visas and American clothing, it's fairly easy to get by customs. But the Mexican federales have been watching us lately. Can you use your powers to tell me if they are watching us now?"

The last thing I wanted to do was help Victor, but if the police raided the house, I would be caught too. The thought of spending years in a Mexican prison made the decision easy. "Yes," I said. "I will need a quiet, dark room and a candle."

Victor set me up in an upstairs bedroom. With the severity of the situation and fear for my life, I quickly entered my dream trance. I flew in my condor body and searched desperately up and down the nearby streets for any sign of the police, but I saw nothing unusual. I told Victor that the coast appeared to be clear, and a few minutes later a group of college-age men came, took the backpacks lined with cocaine, and left a large quantity of money.

I spent a sleepless night in a bedroom Victor provided for me, and in the morning I called Marisol. Much to my relief, she asked to speak to Huitzilopochtli. I knew she would have some kind of a plan by now, and if there was anyone that could talk Huitzilopochtli into doing something, it would be her. More than likely she had secretly taken something of Victor's and dreamt with it that night. Overhearing Victor talking with

Marisol, it was clear that she had succeeded in inviting him to a friend's place to show him something "important." But from the way I saw him look at her the night before, I guessed he would have gone no matter what the invitation. Marisol simply had that kind of power. To my dismay, Victor placed a loaded 9mm pistol in the back of his jeans and covered it with his shirt as we left the house.

I was not surprised that the address Marisol had given to Huitzilopochtli was a botanica (a small shop that sells healing herbs, roots, medicines, amulets, incense, etc.), and as we entered the shop I instantly began to feel less tense. It was the complete opposite of the illegal drug house run by racist extremists where I had just spent the night. Victor seemed totally comfortable and greeted Marisol warmly.

She led us to the back of the shop and through a doorway covered by a single cloth curtain. The room was dark except for a few candles, and I wasn't able to see well until my eyes had adjusted. As I was thinking that, a dark figure stepped quickly out from the corner of the room and did something to Victor that made him collapse almost immediately. The dark figure and Marisol picked him up and placed him in a chair in the center of the room, where they then quickly and efficiently strapped his arms and legs to the chair, which seemed to be securely bolted to the floor.

When my eyes finally adjusted, I wasn't surprised to see that the dark figure was Don Julio, who had come to help us. The only real question I had was whether this was Don Julio in the flesh or his dreaming body that had flown here from Catemaco.

In thinking about it briefly, I decided that it really didn't matter, so I kept my questions to myself.

"Some case you got involved in this time, James," Don Julio said. "I've never seen anything like it in all my years."

"But we've dealt with spirit possession many times before. What makes this so different, and what did you do to Victor?" I asked.

"I gave him a small breath of the brujo de muerte," he replied. "He'll wake up in a few minutes. But this case is special, because Marisol saw in her dreaming that Victor is actually possessed by the spirit of an Aztec warrior that Victor lived as in a past life. So in many ways the spirit that is possessing Victor is actually Victor."

My mind started spinning as to the implications of what Don Julio was saying. He was correct in the fact that I had never dealt with anything like this before. Normally spirits that possess people are foreign entities and not spirits from a previous life. I hadn't even considered this situation before, or if it was even possible that it could actually happen.

Sensing my confusion, Don Julio explained, "As you know, in our system of beliefs we identify three souls. The yolia gives us our rationality, conscience, emotion, deeply felt thoughts, taste, smell, and human characteristics. The tonalli is our heat energy, the fire that animates the body, an impersonal force fueled by the breath. And the nagualli is our double, our alter ego, manifested in the underworld as an animal. The yolia never dies, but when we are conceived in the womb we are imbued with a new and unique tonalli and nagualli in each lifetime. Because of our new tonalli and nagualli, we generally don't remember our previous yolias. However, in Victor's case, one of the previous incarnations of his yolia has come back to him and must be removed so his yolia in this incarnation can live as it was meant to be. His past yolia does not belong here in his waking consciousness, especially if he can't control it."

Victor began to wake up as I told Don Julio and Marisol what I had seen at the house, and Marisol told me what she saw in her dreams as she placed three chairs in front of Victor for us to sit in. Feeling his restraints, Victor became belligerent, as expected. He spat at us and screamed, "How dare you attempt to capture me! I am Huitzilopochtli! I will have all three of your heads on my altar. You cowards! Set me free and fight like men!"

"You are not Huitzilopochtli," Marisol said calmly. "You are obviously a great Aztec warrior, but you are not Huitzilopochtli, for he is a god—and you are no god. Tell us who you really are."

"My people gave me the name Huitzilopochtli out of respect. Before that my name was Manauia; I am the defender. I come here to defend and restore what is ours that the mighty war machine of the Americans has stolen from us. They have taken our lands and treat us as slaves and criminals. We are La Raza, the chosen race, and we will return to glory!"

"Maybe so," said Don Julio, "but not today. And not in the body of the boy you have taken. We want Victor back, and we're not leaving here without him."

"You are fools! You know nothing! Victor is right here. I am Victor, and Victor is me. I did not take him. He called me from the spirit realm to help him when he was at the top of the pyramid of the sun. You cannot separate us, for we have never been apart. Victor was me, Manauia, five hundred years ago, and I am him now. That is our destiny. You cannot change that."

Don Julio motioned us to follow him out to the shop. "We must not argue with Manauia about Victor, because we will never change his mind. He is living once again in a young and strong physical body, and it's true that he and Victor share parts of their yolia and that Victor called him of his own free will. But Victor is still just a boy, and at his age he is bound to do rash things. We must separate Manauia from Victor. Victor deserves to live his own life, not the life of Manauia. The problem is that right now Victor probably doesn't want to be free from Manauia, he's living *la vida loca* and loving it—the excitement, the danger, the women, and working for the freedom of his people. We need to give him a glimpse of his future if he continues on this path, and there is only one way I know to do that."

Don Julio suggested that I fly with Victor to the cave of Mictlan on the wings of the ceratocaula and show him his future in the fire. "If he willingly agrees that what he sees in the future is not what he wants, then you can remove the yolia of Manauia from him. But first we have to get Manauia to agree to the flight."

"But Don Julio, you said I was to fly to Mictlan with Victor, so why do we need Manauia to agree? And how do I separate Victor from Manauia?" I asked.

"Oh, yes," Don Julio replied. "I forgot you did not know this one very important thing. You will use the ceratocaula to fly because the ceratocaula will only work on the true yolia, tonalli, and nagualli of a person in their physical form. Once Manauia-

Victor ingests the ceratocaula, the yolia of Victor will fly with you and be dominant over Manauia. Manauia will still be with you like Victor is still with us now, but with the ceratocaula the yolia of the physical body—in this case, Victor—will be in control. That's why the ceratocaula is necessary in this case."

The three of us walked back into the room and sat down. "We have decided to honor you with a little present," Don Julio said to Manauia. "How would you like to see your future?"

"I don't trust you, old man," he replied, "and I don't trust her either," he said, looking at Marisol. "You are evil witches who put a spell on me and bound me."

"Manauia, if you comply, I will take you," I said. "I promise to show you the future, with no tricks. Wouldn't you like to know what is going to happen in the future? Not many men ever get a chance like this."

A lustful look came over his face. "I comply to go with the tetlachihuic Ulu Temay to see my future."

Don Julio handed me a jar of the ceratocaula paste. In warrior fashion, and because I knew this would keep Victor and me together during the flight, I unsheathed my obsidian knife and cut a long slit in my palm, which I then covered with the paste. Looking at Manauia, he smiled and turned his palm up. I cut his palm and applied the paste, and, looking him straight in the eye, we clasped hands as our blood mingled together.

I told him that in a few minutes we would feel a strong wind and be blown away. When that happened, he was to stay close to me until we landed at a secret cave. Manauia said nothing but seemed to be enjoying himself immensely.

The ceratocaula took us, and after a short flight we arrived at Mictlan. Victor looked around frantically. "Where is Manauia? What have you done?"

"Manauia is still with you, but you are in charge for now," I replied. "It's nice to finally meet you," I added.

"Yeah, whatever," Victor said, and I was glad to actually hear Victor's voice and not Manauia's.

We walked into the cave of the dead. "Fire!" I commanded, and a small but bright fire appeared in the center of the cave floor. I motioned to Victor to sit down, and we both sat staring into the fire.

"I'm curious," I said to Victor. "Are you aware of all the bad things you've been doing—the guns and drugs and stealing?"

"Yeah, so? We are on a mission to reclaim Aztlán. That is all that matters."

"Well, I have news for you, buddy," I said in my evilest voice that didn't even come close to Marisol's but was still effective. "Here in the cave of the dead, the fire can show you what's going to happen if you stay with your hero Manauia. Look closely."

I could see what Victor was seeing, and it wasn't pretty. The fire showed Victor and his friends in a bloody gun fight with Mexican police. Three of his crew lost their lives, and Victor was seriously injured but not killed. The next vision was of him being in court in a prison jumpsuit and chained at the hands and ankles. The vision then jumped to a Mexican news program where the woman reporter announced, "Jailed in Mexico City today, Victor de la Cruz faces multiple charges of racketeering, drug trafficking, weapons possession, and money laundering—

how much money remains to be seen—as well as conspiracy charges in California that carry a life sentence."

"That's bullshit, man," Victor said angrily as he looked up from the fire to me. "Manauia will get me out of all that. He's a supernatural spirit. Those judges and lawyers have no control over him."

"That may be true," I replied. "They cannot control him, but they can control you. *Look!*"

Victor looked back to the fire and saw himself as an old, emaciated man in a dark and dirty jail cell. His hair, teeth, and pride had all left him long go. He was a pitiful shell of a man that wished death would come quickly, as life no longer had any meaning.

He looked at me from across the fire with tears in his eyes.

"Manauia had no more use for you once you went to jail," I said curtly. "You got sent to a maximum-security prison with the scum of humanity as a nineteen-year-old college student, nothing more. Manauia deserted you, and without him, you became the plaything of the prison. You were raped and beaten by multiple men every day for years. You became a slave and lost your identity and dignity. The only reason the inmates didn't kill you was because you were so handsome and fresh."

Looking back into the fire, we both saw the last vision. It was of Victor being buried in a grave outside the prison and no one coming to mourn. His parents had died years before, and he was long forgotten by anyone else.

Victor was sobbing now, but it was not my job to console him. I had to push even more and get Manauia away from him for good.

"Is that the future you want?" I pressed him.

"No."

"Then are you ready to send Manauia away?"

"But what about the cause? My people are being persecuted by the people of the United States and their government."

"Then fight back," I replied. "But fight fire with fire. Get your education and fight legal action with legal action. Win elections, write new laws. Rally your people to freedom without violence or drugs. That is the only way that you and they will ever be truly free."

Finally seeing the resolution on his face, I took out a piece of amatl and scissors from my bag. "Hey, Manauia, show yourself," I commanded.

A wind immediately blew into the cave, and a shadow was cast on the cave wall. Victor drew back from it in fright. I cut the shadow figure into the amatl, and as soon as I was finished it became alive and writhed around in my hands trying to escape. I carefully handed it to Victor.

"You can change the future you just saw, right here and right now. But you have to send Manauia back where he belongs. You must tell him to never return and throw his spirit into the fire."

Victor immediately did as I said and threw Manauia into the fire as if the paper figure burned his hands like acid. A strong wind blew the fire, and the shadow spirit of Manauia left the cave. The wind of Manauia was so strong that it blew the fire completely out. All went dark.

———

Victor and I both remained unconscious until the next day, and when we woke up, Victor's parents were there, and they happily took him home. In the following days, it was decided that Victor could not safely remain in Mexico or the United States because his "colleagues" in La Raza would never accept the change in him or believe or care that he was possessed by a spirit.

Victor ended up attending a university in Canada under a new name, and the last I heard, he was majoring in political science and getting excellent grades.

———

epilogue

Someday I may live permanently in the Tuxtlas with the flying witches of Veracruz. However, after my training with them was complete, I came back to the United States and shortly thereafter moved from Arizona to live amongst the giant sequoias in Northern California, some of the oldest and largest beings on the planet, where I still live now. Here among these ancient entities I have found a very unique and humbling energy that is both rooted and soars toward the sky.

As of the publication of this book, Don Vicente has gone back to the earth and lies in the jungle graveyard of our teachers. Don Julio continues his practice, and Florinda has a new apprentice, a young relative of Marisol who promises to be another awesome flying witch. Marisol seamlessly took over her father's position in the community and is one of the most respected and sought-after curanderas in all of Mexico. She inherited her father's house, where she practices and lives, and I visit her whenever I can or when she asks for assistance with a major situation.

I continue my exploration into alternate realities, working with clients and groups and documenting my experiences. Recently I have reconnected and further deepened my relationship with my Huichol dreaming teachers, the songs of the peyote and the synesthesia that accompanies these experiences. But yet again, that is another story ...

Many blessings on your journey,

James Endredy
BIG TREES, CA

GET MORE AT **LLEWELLYN.COM**

Visit us online to browse hundreds of our books and decks, plus sign up to receive our e-newsletters and exclusive online offers.

- **Free tarot readings • Spell-a-Day • Moon phases**
- **Recipes, spells, and tips • Blogs • Encyclopedia**
- **Author interviews, articles, and upcoming events**

GET SOCIAL WITH **LLEWELLYN**

Find us on
Facebook
www.Facebook.com/LlewellynBooks

Follow us on
twitter
www.Twitter.com/Llewellynbooks

GET BOOKS AT **LLEWELLYN**

LLEWELLYN ORDERING INFORMATION

Order online: Visit our website at www.llewellyn.com to select your books and place an order on our secure server.

Order by phone:
- Call toll free within the US at 1-877-NEW-WRLD (1-877-639-9753)
- Call toll free within Canada at 1-866-NEW-WRLD (1-866-639-9753)
- We accept VISA, MasterCard, and American Express

Order by mail:
Send the full price of your order (MN residents add 6.875% sales tax) in US funds, plus postage and handling, to: Llewellyn Worldwide, 2143 Wooddale Drive, Woodbury, MN 55125-2989

POSTAGE AND HANDLING

STANDARD (US & Canada):
(Please allow 12 business days)
$25.00 and under, add $4.00.
$25.01 and over, FREE SHIPPING.

INTERNATIONAL ORDERS (airmail only): $16.00 for one book, plus $3.00 for each additional book.

Visit us online for more shipping options.
Prices subject to change.

FREE CATALOG!

To order, call
1-877-
NEW-WRLD
ext. 8236
or visit our
website

BEYOND 2012

JAMES ENDREDY

A Shaman's Call to Personal Change and the
Transformation of Global Consciousness

Beyond 2012

A Shaman's Call to Personal Change
and the Transformation of Global Consciousness

James Endredy

War, catastrophic geologic events, Armageddon...the prophecies surrounding 2012—the end of the Mayan calendar—aren't pretty. James Endredy pierces the doom and gloom with hope and a positive, hopeful message for humankind.

For wisdom and guidance concerning this significant date, Endredy consults Tataiwari (Grandfather Fire) and Nakawe (Grandmother Growth)—the "First Shamans." Recorded here is their fascinating dialogue. They reveal how the evolution of human consciousness, sustaining the earth, and our personal happiness are all interconnected.

Discover what you can do to spur the transformation of human consciousness. See how connecting with our true selves, daily acts of compassion and love, focusing personal energy, and even gardening can make a difference. Endredy also shares shamanistic techniques to revive the health of our planet...and ourselves.

978-0-7387-1158-4, 240 pp., 7¹/₂ x 9¹/₈ $16.95

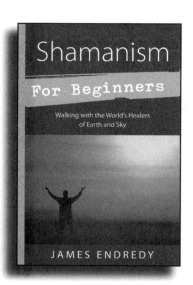

Shamanism

For Beginners

Walking with the World's Healers
of Earth and Sky

JAMES ENDREDY

Shamanism for Beginners

Walking with the World's Healers of Earth and Sky

James Endredy

nterest in shamanism is on the rise, and people are eager to integrate this intriguing tradition into their own lives. *Shamanism for Beginners* introduces the spiritual beliefs and customs of the shaman—a spiritual leader, visionary, healer, diviner, walker between worlds, and so much more.

How is one called to be a shaman? How is a shaman initiated? Where does a shaman's power come from? Exploring the practices and beliefs of tribes around the world, James Endredy sheds light on the entire shamanic experience. The fascinating origins and evolution of shamanism are examined, along with power places, tools (costume, drum, sweat lodge, medicine wheel), sacred plants, and the relationship between the shaman and spirits. Enriched with the author's personal stories and quotes from actual shaman elders and scholars, Endredy concludes with incredible feats of shamans, healing techniques, and ruminations on the future of this remarkable tradition.

978-0-7387-1562-9, 288 pp., 5³/₁₆ x 8 $14.95

———

To Order, Call 1-877-NEW-WRLD

Prices subject to change without notice

ORDER AT LLEWELLYN.COM 24 HOURS A DAY, 7 DAYS A WEEK!

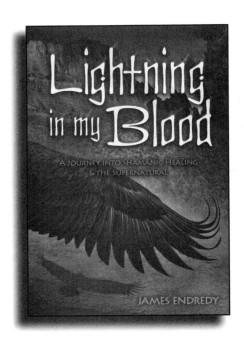

Lightning in my Blood

A Journey into Shamanic Healing & the Supernatural

JAMES ENDREDY

Lightning in My Blood

A Journey into Shamanic Healing & the Supernatural

James Endredy

James Endredy invites you on a wondrous journey into the shape-shifting, mind-altering, and healing magic of shamanism. For decades, Endredy has worked with wise tribal elders around the world, participating in their sacred ceremonies and learning from powerful animal guides and spirits. Here he relives these profound experiences, including his first meeting with a spirit guide that led to the seer's path, a terrifying lesson in using his ethereal body in the Sierra Madre Mountains, how he outwitted an evil sorceress, and his incredible inauguration into shamanic healing.

Grouped by shamanic medicines, Endredy's captivating accounts highlight a fascinating tradition and the extraordinary journey of a modern shaman.

978-0-7387-2147-7, 240 pp., 6 x 9 $16.95

to write to the author

If you wish to contact the author or would like more information about this book, please write to the author in care of Llewellyn Worldwide, and we will forward your request. Both the author and the publisher appreciate hearing from you and learning of your enjoyment of this book and how it has helped you. Llewellyn Worldwide cannot guarantee that every letter written to the author will be answered, but all will be forwarded. Please write to:

James Endredy
c/o Llewellyn Worldwide
2143 Wooddale Drive
Woodbury, MN 55125-2989
Please enclose a self-addressed stamped envelope for reply,
or $1.00 to cover costs. If outside the USA, enclose an
international postal reply coupon.

Many of Llewellyn's authors have websites with additional information and resources. For more information, please visit our website:

HTTP://WWW.LLEWELLYN.COM